THE BEATLES

THE STORIES BEHIND THE SONGS 1962-1966

Steve Turner

CARLTON
BOOKS

782.4216
Tur

This book is dedicated to the memory of
T-Bone Burnett and Larry Norman in memory
of many hours of Beatle-talk over the years.

THIS IS A CARLTON BOOK

First published by Carlton Books Limited 1994
This edition published by
Carlton Books Limited 2009

Text copyright © Steve Turner 1994, 1999,
2005, 2009
Design copyright © Carlton Books Limited
1994, 1999, 2005, 2009

ISBN 978 1 84732 267 8

A CIP catalogue record for this book is
available from the British Library

Printed and bound in China

Managing Art Director: Lucy Coley
Design: Barbara Zuñiga
Executive editor: Rod Green
Editor: Ian Gittins
Picture research: Paul Langan
Production: Claire Hayward

COPYRIGHT CREDITS

'Baby, Let's Play House', words and music by
Arthur Gunter © Williamson Music Inc./Carlin
Music Inc.
'I'm Wishing', words and music by Larry Morey
and Frank Churchill; and 'Please', words and music
by Leo Robbin and Ralph Rainger © Warner
Chappell Music Ltd, London. Reproduced by kind
permission of International Music Publications Ltd.
The songs of the Beatles, words and music by
John Lennon and Paul McCartney or George
Harrison © Northern Songs. Reproduced by kind
permission of Music Sales Group Ltd.

PICTURE CREDITS

The publishers would like to thank the following
sources for their kind permission to reproduce
the pictures in this book.

Corbis: /Bettmann: 35, 61, 74, 115, 169, 176, 180;
/CAT'S: 107, 179; /Waltraud Grubitzsch/epa: 15; /
HO/epa: 18; /Hulton-Deutsch Collection: 26, 46,
51; /John Springer Collection: 72; /Michael Ochs
Archives: 157
Getty Images: /CBS Photo Archive: 32; /Express
Newspapers: 110; /Hulton Archive: 125, 165; /
Keystone: 58, 81, 134; /John Loengard/Time & Life
Pictures: 102; /Rolls Press/Popperfoto: 67; /Bob
Whitaker: 118, 133
PA Photos: /AP: 29, 37, 42, 54, 56, 63, 78, 87,
89, 99, 101, 108, 127, 136, 138, 147, 148, 151,
158, 166; /Allaction.co.uk/Empics Entertainment:
7, 82, 128, 131; /Alpha General: 84; /Barratts:
91, 142, 155; /Bob Daugherty/AP: 93; /Empics
Entertainment: 120; /PA Archive: 8, 11, 12-13, 17,
21, 23, 24, 31, 39, 40, 53, 64, 71, 77, 95, 96, 104, 112,
117, 122, 140, 152, 174; /Sport and General: 69
Rex Features: 160, 162; /Denis Cameron: 48; /
Keystone USA: 145; /David Magnus: 45; /Bill
Orchard: 171, 172

Every effort has been made to acknowledge
correctly and contact the source and/or copyright
holder of each picture and Carlton Books
Limited apologises for any unintentional errors
or omissions, which will be, corrected in future
editions of the book.

CONTENTS

PREFACE

This book tells the stories behind the Beatles' songs, which I've defined as songs written and recorded by the Beatles. It looks at the how, why and where of the songwriting and traces the inspiration back to source.

Having said that, this is not a book about how the Beatles recorded the songs, nor about who played what on which sessions. Mark Lewisohn has done that job definitively in *The Complete Beatles Recording Sessions*. Neither is it a book of in-depth musical analysis. For this approach, see *Twilight Of The Gods* by Professor Wilfrid Mellers (Schirmer Books, 1973) or *The Songwriting Secrets Of The Beatles* by Dominic Pedler (Omnibus Press, 2003).

Also exemplary is *Revolution in the Head* by Ian MacDonald (Fourth Estate, 1994). MacDonald takes the same song-by-song approach that this book takes and his insights and depth of knowledge about popular music of the sixties are unparalleled.

This is also not a book that explains what the Beatles 'were really trying to say'. Although I've given outlines of many songs and have referred to psychological factors that I believe influenced the standpoint of the writing, I've left the task of interpretation to others. If you do

want to know what Paul was saying, read a book like *Paul McCartney: From Liverpool To Let It Be* by Howard DeWitt (Horizon Books, 1992) or, if you want to catch the drift of John's intellectual development, read *The Art and Music of John Lennon* by John Robertson (Omnibus, 1990) or *John Lennon's Secret* by David Stuart Ryan (Kozmik Press, 1982).

What I have tried to do is simply to tell the story of how each song came into being. It could have been a musical inspiration, such as trying to write in the style of Smokey Robinson. It could have been a phrase that just wouldn't go away, like the 'waves of sorrow, pools of joy' line that compelled John to write 'Across The Universe'. Or it could have been an incident like the death of socialite Tara Browne which led to the writing of a section of 'A Day In The Life'.

My primary source has been the words of the Beatles themselves. I was fortunate enough to meet John, interviewing him and Yoko at the Apple office in Savile Row in the summer of 1971, shortly before *Imagine* was released. I remember complimenting him on the personal nature of his new songs that had come after an intense period of therapy. "My songs have always been personal," he responded. "'Help!'

was personal. 'You've Got To Hide Your Love Away' was personal. 'I'm A Loser' was personal. I've always been on that kick.''

I didn't meet Paul until 1992 when I was asked to help Linda in the writing of the text for her photographic book *Linda McCartney's Sixties: Portrait Of An Era*. I had hoped that Paul would contribute his own memories but he decided that he couldn't just dip into a project like this and yet didn't have the time to make a full commitment. He did, however, point out some discrepancies in the stories I had collected so far which I was then able to change.

The most reliable comments on the songs being those made by the Beatles themselves, I've drawn extensively on the published interviews I have personally collected since beginning my first Beatles' scrapbook in 1963. Those that I had missed, I searched out at the National Newspaper Library and the National Sound Archives in London. There were seven invaluable written accounts which I found myself coming back to repeatedly and without which I wouldn't have known where to start. In order of publication these were: Alan Aldridge's interview with Paul McCartney published as *A Good Guru's Guide To The Beatles' Sinister Songbook* in the *Observer* magazine, London, on November 26, 1967; *The Beatles* by Hunter Davies, 1968; *Lennon: The Greatest Natural Songwriter of our Time* by Mike Hennessey in *Record Mirror*, October 2, 1971 (reprinted in *Hit Parade*, April 1972); *Lennon Remembers* by Jann Wenner, 1971; *I Me Mine* by George Harrison, 1980, *The Playboy Interviews* with John Lennon and Yoko Ono, 1981 and *Paul McCartney: Many Years From Now* by Barry Miles (1997). There were also two radio series which shed light on the songwriting: Mike Read's *McCartney*

On McCartney, broadcast on BBC Radio 1 during 1989, and *The Lost Lennon Tapes*, an American production featuring demo tapes from John's private collection which Yoko had allowed to be broadcast for the first time.

As informative as all these were, they didn't tell me the whole story. Many of the anecdotes are already well known. I wanted to interview the people who were around when the songs were written, or who had even been the subject of songs. I also wanted to track down the newspaper stories which had provided ideas, the books from which they'd taken lines and the places which had inspired them. I wanted to surprise even the remaining Beatles themselves because I knew that they didn't know who Mr Kite really was or what happened to the girl whose story inspired 'She's Leaving Home'.

The definitive book on this subject won't be written until John's and George's journals, letters and work books are made public and Paul and Ringo sit down in front of a microphone and share everything they remember about the 208 songs which the Beatles recorded. The chances are, though, that John's material will remain locked in vaults for the foreseeable future because much of it refers to people still living and Yoko believes that it is too sensitive to release. The six-part television series *The Beatles Anthology* and the accompanying 'biography' of the Beatles was disappointing to anyone expecting the remaining members of the Beatles to tell hitherto-untold stories.

That's why it was worth compiling this book. It may be the closest we'll ever get to understanding how the Beatles conjured up their songwriting magic.

Steve Turner
London, November 1998 and March 2005

INTRODUCTION

I once worked out that if you added up the number of days that the Beatles existed as recording artists, the midpoint of their career came when John Lennon had to defend himself over his comparison between the group and Jesus. It was a highly symbolic half way post because it marked the beginning of the end of their life as a touring act and their transition from highly polished practitioners of show business into serious artists. It also marked the beginning of their life as spokesmen for a generation.

The songs explored in this book are all from the first half of their lives together on record; the period largely characterised by Beatlemania, concert tours, Cuban heel boots, hair on foreheads (but not faces) and songs that were hummable and predominantly about boys who liked girls or girls who liked boys. It starts with the quintessential Merseybeat sound of 'I Saw Her Standing There' and ends with the contemplative and vaguely druggy *Rubber Soul* album.

When the Beatles first went into EMI's Abbey Road Studios in 1962, their ambitions were no greater than any other group that had grown up on rock'n'roll. They wanted to produce good, catchy songs that would get them into the pop charts and make them money. Their role model was Elvis. Three years later, when they cut *Rubber Soul*, they'd already topped Elvis and made their fortune. They were now more interested in Ravi Shankar, states of altered consciousness and being appreciated as artists.

John Lennon and Paul McCartney were the first major pop stars to have benefited from an extended education. Before the Beatles, pop music was a career for those who'd failed in academia and fancied their chances at making it on their looks and voices alone. Although John never excelled in exams and aborted his art studies, he had at least been to college. Paul hadn't been to college but he'd been to one of the best grammar schools in Liverpool and had studied for his A-levels.

The difference this made was that, as time went on, they were able to see what they did as musicians and composers as being like what Chaucer, Picasso and Dylan Thomas had done. They could identify with the creative approaches if these artists and the battles they fought to extend the scope of their art forms. In 1963 John made the prescient comment: "This isn't show business. It's something else. This is different from anything that anybody imagines. You don't go on from this. You do this, and then you finish."

The early songs in their catalogue were not lyrically profound although they were invariably musically complex, always adding fresh chord changes and key shifts that they'd learned from an obscure

"Here are a few that we made earlier": the Beatles compare and contrast the sleeves to some of their peerless music catalogue.

record or an older more experienced musician. They consciously worked within the expectations of the existing pop market and took their cues from already successful songs that they would atomise to discover how they worked. "We were just writing pop songs a la Everly Brothers, a la Buddy Holly," John once explained. "They were pop songs with no more thought to them than…to create a sound. And the words were almost irrelevant."

When they started there was no thought of being confessional or of exploring the world of ideas. There were times when events suggested storylines but the influences were much more likely to come from other songs than from events in their lives. John later admitted that he kept his personal observations and experiments in language for his poems and short stories. Some of these were later published in his two books, *In His Own Write* and *A Spaniard in the Works.* "I was already a stylised songwriter on the first album," he said. "To express myself I would write…personal stories which expressed my personal emotions. I'd have a separate, songwriting John Lennon who wrote songs for the sort of meat market, and I didn't consider the lyrics to have any depth at all. They were just a joke."

When the Beatles dressed in black leather and played in cellar clubs their sets were dominated by songs recorded by Elvis, Buddy Holly, Gene Vincent, Little Richard and the Everly Brothers. Later they developed an interest in American girl groups such as the Shirelles and the Chiffons and the new Motown sound of the Miracles and Marvin Gaye. The songwriting team they admired the most was Gerry Goffin and Carole King, the authors of hits like 'Will You Still Love Me Tomorrow,' 'Chains,' 'One Fine Day,' 'Take Good Care Of My Baby,' and 'Please Don't Ever Change.'

"First of all, Paul and I wanted to be the Goffin and King of England," said John, and in their early compositions it's possible to see the hallmarks of the Brill Building school of songwriting where hits were written to order during a normal eight-hour day. Like Goffin and King, John and Paul began to write for other artists, offering 'World Without Love,' 'Nobody I Know' and 'I Don't Want To See You Again' to Peter and Gordon, 'Bad To Me' and 'Do You Want To Know A Secret' to Billy J. Kramer and the Dakotas.

Artists clamoured to cover Lennon/McCartney songs. As soon as demo discs were sent to publisher Dick James they were passed on to relevant artists. By 1965 almost every song on a Beatles' album

The band pictured at EMI's headquarters at Manchester Square, London, with a host of silver discs. Even by 1963, the band were setting sales records.

would end up being covered by someone, some of them, like 'Michelle' by the Overlanders, becoming hits in their own right.

The first stage in their songwriting extended from their early work as teenagers who would meet regularly at Paul's family home and scribble lyrics in Liverpool Institute exercise books through the rise of Beatlemania.

By 1964, things were already beginning to change. As they travelled more widely and began mixing with the elite of the young London arts world, their horizons began to extend. Hearing Bob Dylan's early albums showed them the potential within pop and rock to deal with a wider range of emotions and to be more daring with language. It led John to write such soul-baring songs as 'I'm a Loser,' and 'Help.' Dylan showed him how it was possible to carry the spirit of his poetry and creative writing into song.

Paul was affected in different ways. Through his actress girlfriend Jane Asher and her family he was introduced to classical musicians, psychologists, actors, theatre directors, poets and members of London's fledgling 'underground' scene. He visited art galleries, made home movies, experimented with electronic music, went to the theatre and attended lectures. The exposure to a broader range of ideas and art forms was evidenced in the new maturity of songs like 'And I Love Her,' 'We Can Work It Out' and 'Yesterday.'

What made the Beatles' development so exciting during this period was their refusal to be restricted by the limitations routinely accepted by pop musicians. They introduced new instruments (Hammond organ and African drum on *Beatles For Sale*, electric piano, flutes and string quartet on *Help!*, sitar and fuzz bass on *Rubber Soul*), tackled new subjects and incorporated happy accidents into their music.

The band exceeded the normal recording levels, defied the received wisdom on album covers (rarely a smile and not even their name on the front of *Rubber Soul*) and expected producer George Martin to realise their wildest conceptions.

On each album they extended the boundaries of pop, creating the foundation for all pop that has followed. They were blessed with boundless optimism. If they could conceive something in their minds they saw no reason why it couldn't be actualised. It's no accident that the lyric most closely associated with them in these years was 'Yeah! Yeah! Yeah!' For the Beatles, everything seemed attainable.

The mid-Sixties saw a quantum leap in both the musical ideas and lyrical scope of the Beatles' music as they matured as artists.

They began, tentatively at first, to write songs that weren't about love. Although 'In My Life' featured the word love it was really about intimations of mortality. 'Help' was a cry of desolation. 'Nowhere Man' ruminated on the meaning of life. 'The Word,' on *Rubber Soul*, was the group's first 'message song.' They'd reached the point where they were being looked to for guidance and they responded appropriately.

"This is who we are now," said Paul shortly after the album's release. "People have always wanted us to stay the same, but we can't stay in a rut. No one else expects to hit a peak at 23 and never develop, so why should we? *Rubber Soul*, for me, is the beginning of my adult life."

The three year journey from *Please Please Me* to *Rubber Soul* was the most extraordinary in 20th century pop and we're still coming to terms with the legacy. The northern entertainers who many thought would go the way of Tommy Steele and the Hula Hoop instead became one of the most powerful creative forces in modern music. Faddish songs seem hollow once the fad has died out but the pleasure produced by a Beatles song never seems to diminish. They still have the ability to amaze, fascinate and disturb.

It's because of this power that we're constantly drawn to know more about them and where they came from.

Overleaf: They may have matured into the most ferocious creative minds in popular music but the Beatles began life as happy-go-lucky, chirpy Northern lads.

11

PLEASE PLEASE ME

One of the great strengths of the Beatles was that by 1962, the year they cut their first record, they were already seasoned performers, well-versed in American soul, gospel, rhythm and blues and rock'n'roll. Most of what they knew had been learned the hard way. They knew how songs were constructed because, unable to afford sheet music, they had to decipher lyrics and work out chord changes by listening to records over and over again. Having played rock'n'roll to adoring teenagers at the lunch-time Cavern Club sessions in Liverpool, as well as to inebriated German businessmen in Hamburg, they also knew how to excite, calm and seduce an audience.

John and Paul had been together for five years; George had been with them for almost as long. Ringo was a recent member, having replaced Pete Best on drums, but they'd known him since 1959 and his previous position with Rory Storm and the Hurricanes meant that he had played the same venues as they had.

At this time, the Beatles' material was standard beat group fare – the best-known songs by the best-known rock'n'roll artists. Top of their list was Elvis Presley. They covered almost 30 of the songs he'd recorded, as well as numbers by Chuck Berry, Buddy Holly, Carl Perkins, Gene Vincent, Fats Domino, Jerry Lee Lewis, Larry Williams, Ray Charles, the Coasters, Arthur Alexander, Little Richard and the Everly Brothers. Studying the music of these artists taught John and Paul the basics of songwriting.

When they came together at Paul's house to write their own material, it was a case of reassembling the familiar chords and words to make something distinctively theirs. This is how a bass riff from a Chuck Berry number came to be incorporated into 'I Saw Her

Please Please Me hit Number 1 in Britain but failed to chart in the US, where it was went under the name *Introducing The Beatles*.

Standing There', a song about seeing a girl at the Tower Ballroom in New Brighton, and explains how the sound of Roy Orbison's voice came to be the inspiration behind 'Please Please Me', the Beatles' first Number 1 single.

Sometimes their songs were 'about' incidents from their lives but often the words, like the chords, were borrowed from what had gone before. At this stage, the words were important to create sounds and impressions, rather than to convey a message.

Most of their debut album was recorded in a single session on February 11, 1963. It was released on March 22, 1963, and reached the top spot in the British charts. In America it was titled *Introducing The Beatles* and released on the little-known Vee Jay label. The US version didn't include 'Please Please Me' or 'Ask Me Why' and failed to make the charts.

I SAW HER STANDING THERE

Producer George Martin's original idea had been to tape a Beatles' show at the Cavern Club in Liverpool but it was later decided to get the group to play their live show in the studio and cut the album in a day. This was done on February 11, 1963, when in a 15-hour session the Beatles recorded ten new tracks to which were added both sides of their first two singles.

'I Saw Her Standing There' was the perfect song with which to open the Beatles' first album because it set the group firmly in the context of sweaty ballrooms, full of dancing teenage girls. They decided to keep the 1-2-3-4 'intro' as this added to the impression of a raw Liverpool beat group captured in live performance.

Originally titled 'Seventeen', the song tells the simple story of a boy who sees a girl dancing at the local ballroom and, after deciding that her looks are 'way beyond compare', determines never to dance with anyone else again. As the story unfolds there is a wonderful

I SAW HER STANDING THERE

Written: Lennon/McCartney
Length: 2' 55"
UK release: *Please Please Me* album, March 22, 1963
US release: *Introducing The Beatles* album, July 22, 1963
US single release: December 26, 1963, as B-side of 'I Want To Hold Your Hand'

'I Saw Her Standing There' set the Beatles firmly in the world of sweaty ballrooms and dancing teenage girls. It was a classic, almost ideal debut single.

mixture of youthful arrogance and insecurity portrayed. There is no hint that the narrator has considered the possibility of rejection and yet, in that unforgettable beat group rhyme, we're told that as he 'crossed the room' his heart 'went boom'.

Paul started composing this song one night in September 1962 while driving back to his home in Allerton, Liverpool. He liked the idea of writing about a 17-year-old girl because he was conscious of the need to have songs which the group's largely female audience could easily relate to. "I didn't think a lot about it as I sang it to myself," he said four years later. "Originally the first two lines were 'She was just seventeen, Never been a beauty queen'. It sounded like a good rhyme to me at the time. But when I played it through to John the next day, I realized that it was a useless line and so did John. So we both sat down and tried to come up with another line which rhymed with 17 but which meant something."

After a while, John came up with 'you know what I mean', which, as Paul recognized, could either be dismissed as a filler or accepted as sexual innuendo, 16 being the legal age of sexual consent. It was also a very Liverpudlian phrase that neatly avoided the borrowed Americanisms which littered most English rock'n'roll of the time.

Mike McCartney photographed his brother and John sitting by the fireplace in Forthlin Road working on this song. Paul was sitting in front of a small black and white television and John was beside him wearing his horn-rimmed spectacles. They were both playing acoustic guitars and a Liverpool Institute exercise book was open in front of them on the floor with the crossings out in the song clearly visible.

Paul later explained in an interview with *Beat Instrumental* that the bass riff was stolen from Chuck Berry's 1961 song 'I'm Talking About You'. "I played exactly the same notes as he did and it fitted

our number perfectly," he confessed. "Even now, when I tell people about it, I find few of them believe me. Therefore, I maintain that a bass riff doesn't have to be original."

In December 1961, Paul had started dating Iris Caldwell, sister of the local beat singer Rory Storm, whose group the Hurricanes featured Ringo Starr as drummer (he joined the Beatles in August 1962). Just like the girl in 'I Saw Her Standing There', Iris was only 17 at the time when Paul saw her dancing the twist at the Tower Ballroom in New Brighton (situated 25 minutes out of Liverpool). She was a trained dancer and Paul was apparently impressed with her legs, which were displayed in fishnet stockings, and the fact that she was already working professionally in show business.

Paul became a frequent guest at the Caldwell family home at 54 Broad Green Road, Liverpool 15, which was known to the local beat groups as Hurricaneville. He became close to Iris' mother, Violet, and would often drop in with John to sit around and write songs. "Paul and I dated for a couple of years," says Iris. "It was never that serious. We never pretended to be true to each other. I went out with lots of people. I was working away in different theatres at the time but if I was back home then we would go out. There were never any promises made or love declared."

According to Iris, Paul intended giving 'I Saw Her Standing There' to her brother Rory to record. "He thought it would be a good song for him but it wasn't dealt out that way. Brian Epstein didn't want Rory to have it."

By late 1962, 'I Saw Her Standing There' was part of the Beatles' stage act, one of the earliest Lennon and McCartney songs slipped between those of Buddy Holly and Little Richard. During the recording at Abbey Road in February 1963 the song was new enough for Paul to sometimes forget the sequence of the verse endings 'How could I dance?', 'She wouldn't dance' and 'I'll never dance'.

The first cover version of the song was by the English rock'n'roll singer Duffy Power in 1963. In America, it became the flip side of 'I Want To Hold Your Hand', the single released in January 1964 that was the Beatles' first US Number 1. It was one of five songs which the Beatles performed on the celebrated *Ed Sullivan Show* of February 9, 1964, which was watched by 70 million people, then the largest US TV audience ever recorded. In November 1974, John performed the song with Elton John at Madison Square Garden.

'I Saw Her Standing There' was one the very first original compositions that the Beatles slipped into their sets alongside rock'n'roll covers

MISERY

By January 1963, with 'Love Me Do' a British Top 20 hit under their belt, the songwriting confidence of the McCartney/Lennon team (as they were initially credited) had grown, but when plans were made to record their first LP, they were suddenly under pressure to come up with some new songs .

Although not all the songs were going to be their own compositions – they had chosen material by American songwriters to fill almost half the album – they were determined to stamp their own mark on the recording and not become yet another British act making a living out of cover versions. In the climate of the times, this was a bold move. Traditionally, British rock'n'roll acts didn't record their own songs but, aping the US sound, covered promising American singles before they were released in the UK. Cliff Richard, Britain's top home-grown pop star when the Beatles signed to EMI , had broken the mould slightly by recording songs written by Ian Samwell, a former member of his backing group, but no one in the UK had succeeded in producing genuinely British-sounding rock'n'roll.

It was against this background that Paul and John began to pull together the five new unreleased songs for their debut album *Please Please Me*. Backstage at the King's Hall, Glebe Street, Stoke-on-Trent, where they were playing a concert on January 26, 1963, they huddled together and wrote 'Misery', with John as the major contributor. Just as Paul had shown unbounded confidence that he would get to dance with the girl in 'I Saw Her Standing There', John kicked off his career as an album artist by complaining about a girl who had left him and made him lonely. 'The world is treating me bad' was the song's portentous first line. "Allan Clarke and Graham Nash of the

Hollies helped on that song," remembers Tony Bramwell, then an employee of Brian Epstein. "John and Paul were desperate to get it finished and got stuck on one of the lines and Allan and Graham began throwing in suggestions. The boys wanted to get it ready for Helen Shapiro."

Allan Clarke can remember the day well but not the lines or words that he helped throw in. "It was just four guys together sitting in a room," he says. "John and Paul were plunking along writing this song and we helped with a couple of words. Everyone thought that the Hollies and the Beatles were in competition with each other but we weren't really."

Within days they had made a tape and sent it to Norrie Paramor of EMI's Columbia label for him to consider for Shapiro, who they

The Beatles took the brave decision to record a debut album composed largely of self-penned material.

MISERY

Written: Lennon/McCartney
Length: 1' 50"
UK release: *Please Please Me* album, March 22, 1963
US single release: *Introducing The Beatles* album, July 22, 1963

knew would shortly be recording in Nashville. Indeed, Paul told Alan Smith, the editor of *New Musical Express*, that it was a song written to be covered: "We've called it 'Misery' but it isn't quite as slow as it sounds. It moves along at quite a steady pace and we think Helen Shapiro will make quite a good job of it."

Just 16 at the time, Helen had been having Top 10 hits in Britain since early 1961 and the Beatles were due to debut on the cinema circuit as one of seven support acts on her 14-date February tour. It would only be in the final shows, with 'Please Please Me' a Top 10 sensation, that the Beatles were upgraded, although even then they only got to close the first half. Package tours still formed part of the British entertainment scene at the time, despite being a hangover from the days of variety shows where singers followed jugglers and magicians on to the stage. For this tour, the Beatles had time to deliver four songs and were sandwiched between comedy turns.

"I got on great with them," remembers Helen, "and John was like a brother to me. Very protective. He and Paul certainly offered 'Misery' to me first, through Norrie, but I didn't know anything about it until I met them on the first day of the tour (February 2, Bradford, Yorks). Apparently he'd turned it down even though I hadn't heard it." The offer was taken up by another artist on the same tour, Kenny Lynch, a black singer from Britain, whose biggest success to date had been a Top 10 hit with a cover of the Drifters' 'Up On The Roof'. 'Misery' wasn't a hit for him but it gave him the distinction of being the first non-Beatle to record a Lennon and McCartney song.

The 'la-la-la-la-la' outro appeared to allude to Pat Boone's 'Speedy Gonzales', a single that had entered the British charts in July 1962 and didn't leave until October.

ASK ME WHY

ASK ME WHY
Written:
Lennon/McCartney
Length: 2' 27"
UK single release:
January 11, 1963
as B-side of 'Please
Please Me'
US single release:
February 25, 1963
as B-side of 'Please
Please Me'

Written in the spring of 1962, with John as the major contributor, 'Ask Me Why' was a lightweight love song from the Beatles' set at the Cavern Club that year, and was premiered on the BBC radio programme *Teenagers' Turn* on June 11, 1962. It was one of four songs which they took to their first recording session on June 6, 1962, at EMI Studios in Abbey Road, north London, but George Martin didn't think it was strong enough to be their debut single. Re-recorded in February 1963, it was released in Britain as the B side of 'Please Please Me'.

'Ask Me Why' was in the running to be the Beatles' debut single but eventually appeared as the B-side of 'Please Please Me'.

PLEASE PLEASE ME

'Please Please Me' was one of those innocent-sounding pop songs with a subversive subtext. Some critics have seen it as a plea for equality in sexual pleasure. Robert Christgau, music editor of New York's *Village Voice*, has more controversially claimed that it's about oral sex. Under pressure in 1967 over alleged drug references in their work Paul commented: "If they had wanted to they could have found plenty of double meanings in our early work. How about 'I'll Keep You Satisfied' or 'Please Please Me'? Everything has a double meaning if you look for it long enough."

Iris Caldwell remembers Paul coming over to her house one night and reading her the words to the just-completed song. "He used to pick up my brother's guitar and play it but that night he didn't bother," she says. "He just read out the lyrics. They didn't seem to make any sense to me at the time and I thought they were absolutely awful." The song's origins were certainly innocuous, the chorus having been suggested by the 1932 Bing Crosby song 'Please', written by Leo Robin and Ralph Rainger, which starts off by playing with the homophones 'pleas' and 'please': 'Oh please, lend your little ear to my pleas, Lend a ray of cheer to my pleas, Tell me that you love me too'. Later, John recalled that his mother, Julia, sang this to him as a child, adding that he'd always been fascinated by the dual use of the 'please' sound.

When John came to write this song, in his front bedroom at 251 Menlove Avenue in Liverpool ("I remember the day and the pink eyelet on the bed"), he imagined Roy Orbison singing it because he'd just been listening to the hit single 'Only The Lonely'. It's easy to imagine Orbison singing the original slow version of 'Please Please

Although some critics claimed that 'Please Please Me' was a song about oral sex, it was originally inspired by a 1932 number sung by Bing Crosby.

Me'. With his pallid, dough-like features and permanent shades, Orbison might have looked an unlikely pop star, but he was a brilliantly soulful singer and wrote his own songs. He was someone whom John in particular could relate to because his lyrics explored dark moods of loss and loneliness – and he wore glasses.

Within months of 'Please Please Me' being released as a single and reaching the Number 2 spot in the British charts, the Beatles were picked to support Orbison on a three-week tour of Britain. "We never talked to each other about songwriting on that tour," remembered Orbison years later. "The basic thing they wanted to know at that time was how I thought they would get on in America. I told them to let people know they were British and to get on something like the Ed Sullivan Show. If they did that, I said they could be just as big in America as they were in Britain. I said that in an article for *New Musical Express* which came out during the tour. I thought it was important that they let people know they were British because we hadn't heard much from Britain except for the Blue Streak missile and the Profumo scandal."

His exact words, recorded in May 1963, were: "The Beatles could well be tops in America. These boys have enough originality to storm our charts with the same effect as they have done here, but it will need careful handling. They have something that is entirely new even to us Americans and although we have an influx of hit groups at home I really do believe they could top the charts...It's a change to see new stars who are not just watered-down versions of Elvis Presley. This seems to be a sound they have made famous all on their own and I really think it is the greatest. Though you know it as

PLEASE PLEASE ME

Written:	Lennon/McCartney
Length:	2' 03"
UK single release:	January 11, 1963
UK chart position:	2
US single release:	February 25, 1963
US chart position:	3

Merseyside music, I am sure this will be hailed as the new British sound in America."

Orbison didn't discover that John had written 'Please Please Me' in emulation of his style until producer George Martin mentioned it to him in June 1987 at an Abbey Road celebration for the 20th anniversary of *Sgt Pepper's Lonely Hearts Club Band*. "He told me that it sounded so much like me that they had to change it a little bit," Orbison commented. "That's a nice thing to find out."

In March 1963 John had revealed that they had intended 'Please Please Me' as a B side for their first single until Martin complained about this similarity. "He thought that the arrangement was fussy, so we tried to make it simpler," said John. "In the weeks following (the 'Love Me Do' session), we went over it again and again. We changed the tempo a little. We altered the words slightly and we went over the idea of featuring the harmonica, just as we'd done in 'Love Me Do'. By the time we came to record it, we were so happy with it that we couldn't wait to get it down."

The Beatles' fondness for Orbison was to survive the Sixties. John described the sound of his last single, 'Starting Over', as 'Elvis Orbison' and in 1988 George Harrison joined Orbison, Bob Dylan, Tom Petty and Jeff Lynne in recording the critically-acclaimed *Traveling Wilburys* album.

The Beatles toured the UK in 1963 as support to Roy Orbison, whose music was influential on them throughout their entire career.

LOVE ME DO

In Britain, 'Love Me Do' was the Beatles' first hit and, like the group's image, it was all pretty strange to a generation which had spent the last two or three years listening to insipid pop performed by men with short haircuts and big grins.

An early song written by Paul, the lyrics of 'Love Me Do' were as basic as could be, with most words consisting of only one syllable and 'love' being repeated 21 times. 'I love you forever so please love me in return' was the song's entire lyrical statement. What set it apart from the teen love songs of the time was a gospel-blues tinge to the singing – a feeling that was heightened by John's harmonica and the slightly mournful close harmonizing. (John's fondness for gospel was confirmed when he listed R&B and gospel as his 'tastes in music' in the *New Musical Express* of February 15, 1963.)

During 1962, the American star Bruce Channel had enjoyed a British hit with 'Hey Baby' which featured a harmonica solo by

---

LOVE ME DO

Written:	Lennon/McCartney
Length:	2' 22"
UK single release:	October 5, 1962
UK chart position:	4
US single release:	April 27, 1964
US chart position:	1

Nashville session musician Delbert McClinton. John was impressed by this and, when he met McClinton in June 1962 at the Tower Ballroom, New Brighton, where the Beatles were playing support for Channel, he asked him how he played it.

"John was very interested in harmonica and, when we went on to play another couple of dates with the Beatles, he and I hung out a lot together," says McClinton. "He wanted me to show him whatever I could. He wanted to know how to play. Before our time together was over he had his own harmonica ready in his pocket." It was only three months later that the Beatles recorded 'Love Me Do', in which John was able to include a distinctive harmonica break.

John went on to play harmonica on the next two singles, 'Please Please Me' and 'With Love From Me To You', as well as on six other tracks including 'Little Child' (*With The Beatles*) and 'I Should Have Known Better' (*A Hard Day's Night*). The last time he used it on record was on 'I'm A Loser' (*Beatles For Sale*) recorded in August 1964. By that time he reckoned it had turned into a Beatles' gimmick.

'Love Me Do' was included on the group's first four-track extended play record which had sleeve notes written by Tony Barrow, a Lancashire journalist who was then working as the Beatles' press officer. Barrow's comments on the four tracks ('From Me To You', 'Thank You Girl', 'Please Please Me' and 'Love Me Do') were remarkably prescient.

"The four numbers on this EP have been selected from *The Lennon and McCartney Songbook*," he wrote. "If that description sounds a trifle pompous perhaps I may suggest you preserve this sleeve for ten years, exhume it from your collection somewhere around the middle of 1973 and write me a very nasty letter if the pop people of the Seventies aren't talking about at least two of these titles as 'early examples of modern beat standards taken from *The Lennon and McCartney Songbook*'."

In 1967, when every Beatle song was believed to be drenched in meaning and they had been elevated into 'spokesmen for a generation', Paul commented to Alan Aldridge in an interview for The *Observer* "'Love Me Do' was our greatest philosophical song... for it to be simple, and true, means that it's incredibly simple."

Even as late as 1967, when they were seen as spiritual gurus to a generation, Paul was calling 'Love Me Do' the Beatles' "greatest philosophical song".

PS I LOVE YOU

Written in 1961, 'PS I Love You' was another early song by Paul which the Beatles considered recording as their first single. In Britain, it became the B-side of 'Love Me Do'. In America, almost two years later, it became a single in its own right and made the Top 10.

It had become fairly routine for British beat groups of the time to play stints in German night clubs, where there was a great demand for the new American-style music but few musicians around who could actually play it. In April 1961, the Beatles – John, Paul, George, Pete Best (drums) and Stuart Sutcliffe (bass) – started a gruelling 13-week residency at the Top Ten Club in Hamburg, Germany, playing for over five hours each night, seven days a week. It was the best apprenticeship they could have had. The continuous playing of other artists' songs taught them how songs were constructed and the pressure to entertain taught them what worked and what didn't.

Paul's girlfriend at the time was Dorothy 'Dot' Rhone, an elfin Liverpool teenager who worked for a chemist and lived at home with her parents. She was a shy but sweet girl whom Paul had been dating for a while and who had become a regular guest at his family home in Liverpool. "She was very much in love with Paul," remembered her friend Sandra Hedges. "He in turn would jealously guard her by placing her amid the group while they were playing." Dot became close to Cynthia Powell, John's girlfriend from art school, and during the Easter holidays the two girls decided to visit their boyfriends in Germany, Cynthia staying with Astrid Kirchner, Stuart Sutcliffe's girlfriend, and Dot staying with Paul on a houseboat.

After Dot had returned to Liverpool, Paul wrote this song which she assumed was for her although, years later, Paul denied that he

PS I LOVE YOU

Written:
Lennon/McCartney
Length: 2' 05''
UK single release:
October 5, 1962
as B-side of 'Love
Me Do'
US single release:
April 27, 1964
as B-side of 'Love
Me Do'

George and the rest of the Beatles, whose line-up still included Pete Best and Stuart Sutcliffe, played a tough 13-week residency in Hamburg in 1961.

had anyone specific in mind. Written in the form of a letter, 'PS I Love You' was the precursor of Paul's other letter songs, 'Paperback Writer' and 'When I'm 64'. Paul's relationship with Dot was picked up after returning from Hamburg but ended in the summer of 1962 just as the Beatles began recording. At the time, she was sharing a flat with John's girlfriend Cynthia Powell at 93 Garmoyle Road, Liverpool, close to Penny Lane.

Paul came round late one night and broke the news to Dot. Cynthia remembered her collapsing in tears. "Poor little defenceless Dot," she wrote in her book *A Twist Of Lennon*. "She wouldn't hurt a fly but had been hurt so much that she couldn't even tell me without renewed convulsions and outbursts of uncontrollable crying. As it happens, she didn't need to tell me anything. Only one thing would have done that to Dot and that was Paul giving her the push...he was too young to settle down. He wanted desperately to be footloose and fancy free and I suppose he let Dot down very gently under the circumstances."

DO YOU WANT TO KNOW A SECRET?

Around the same time that Paul finished with Dot Rhone, Cynthia discovered that she was pregnant. On August 23, 1962, she and John did the conventional thing by getting married at a registry office in Mount Pleasant, Liverpool. The best man at this small affair attended by Paul, George, and a handful of relations was manager Brian Epstein, who offered the newlyweds the privacy of a ground floor flat he rented at 36 Faulkner Street to start their married life. This

'Do You Want To Know A Secret?' was based on a song that John's mother had picked up from Disney's 1937 film *Snow White and the Seven Dwarves*.

**DO YOU WANT
TO KNOW
A SECRET?**
Written:
Lennon/McCartney
Length: 1'59"
UK single release:
Please Please Me
album, March 22,
1963
US single release:
*Introducing The
Beatles* album,
July 22, 1963

wasn't Epstein's main home but a place in the city centre that he kept for his own discreet homosexual liaisons.

Cynthia remembered being ecstatic at the unexpected wedding gift as they hadn't given much thought to where they would live and there was no time in the busy Beatles' schedule for a honeymoon. "It was the first apartment I'd ever had that wasn't shared by 14 other art students," John later admitted.

It was while living here that John wrote 'Do You Want To Know A Secret?', the secret in question being that he had just realized that he was really in love. As with 'Please Please Me', it had its genesis in a song his mother used to sing to him, which she in turn had picked up from Walt Disney's 1937 film *Snow White And The Seven Dwarfs*. In one of the opening scenes in the film, Snow White is working as a kitchen maid and, as she stands by the castle well, she begins to sing to the doves: 'Wanna know a secret?, Promise not to tell?, We are standing by a wishing well' ('I'm Wishing', words and music by Larry Morey and Frank Churchill).

In an interview with *Musician* magazine, George Harrison was later to reveal that the musical inspiration for the song came from 'I Really Love You', a 1961 hit for the Stereos.

John made a demo of 'Do You Want To Know A Secret' on an acoustic guitar while sitting in a bathroom (a fact that became obvious because of the flush of a toilet at the end of the song). This was offered to another Epstein artist, Billy J Kramer, who took it with him to Germany as part of his stage act. Kramer's real name was Billy Ashton and he was Epstein's third signing following on closely from Gerry and the Pacemakers. Epstein then acquired the Big Three, the Fourmost, Tommy Quickly and Cilla Black, all of them Liverpool acts.

Kramer came back from Germany convinced that 'Do You Want To Know A Secret?' wasn't a crowd pleaser but EMI liked it enough to offer him a recording contract after hearing a test tape of it. It went on to become a Number 2 hit for him in Britain during the summer of 1963, the first time a Lennon and McCartney song by another artist had made the Hit Parade.

Although John had written it with his own voice in mind, when the Beatles recorded it, the song was offered to George. "I thought it would be a good vehicle for him," John said, "because it only had three notes and he wasn't the best singer in the world."

33

THERE'S A PLACE

Just as 'Misery' indicated the feelings of isolation and rejection which would become a major preoccupation in John's songs, so 'There's A Place' introduced what was to become a recurring theme of finding comfort in his thoughts, dreams and memories. In 'There's A Place', John deals with his life's sorrow by retreating into the safety of his inner thoughts and, in a more sophisticated way, this is what he would do in later songs such as 'Strawberry Fields Forever', 'Girl', 'In My Life', 'Rain', 'I'm Only Sleeping' and many others. "The usual Lennon thing," he said of 'There's A Place'. "It's all in your mind."

"He was a combination of introversion and extroversion," says Thelma McGough who as Thelma Pickles dated John while they were both at Liverpool School of Art. "He appeared very extrovert and yet it was all front. He was actually very deep but he'd keep that pretty well hidden until you were on your own with him."

Although John spoke as though the song was entirely his, Paul has since claimed that the original idea for it came from him, the title being derived from the *West Side Story* song 'There's A Place For Us' (1957) which he had in his Forthlin Road record collection.

Musically, John admitted that 'There's A Place' was his attempt at "a sort of Motown, black thing", referring to what was then a hot new sound emerging from Detroit on Berry Gordy's fledgling independent record label. Motown hits were mostly written by production line writers and performed by groups trained in the label's own school – it was dance music driven by inventive bass lines, gospel-style splashes of tambourine and vocal harmonies. Among the Beatles' favourite acts were Barrett Strong, the Miracles (featuring Smokey Robinson), the Marvelettes, Marvin Gaye and 'Little' Stevie Wonder.

In fact the Beatles were to play a crucial role in popularizing the Motown label, initially by recording Motown songs such as 'Please Mr Postman', 'You've Really Got A Hold On Me' and 'Money' and later by dropping the names of new Motown artists and records in interviews. Explaining the success of his label to *Record World* in 1964 Berry Gordy said: "It helped when we had several songs of ours recorded by the Beatles. I met them and found out that they were great fans of Motown and had been studying Motown music, and they went on to become some of the greatest songwriters in history. We were absolutely delighted."

The Beatles' early image could be comedic but 'There's A Place' had a depth that belied their slapstick antics.

THERE'S A PLACE

Written:	Lennon/McCartney
Length:	1' 52"
UK release:	*Please Please Me* album, March 22, 1963
US release:	*Introducing The Beatles* album, July 22, 1963

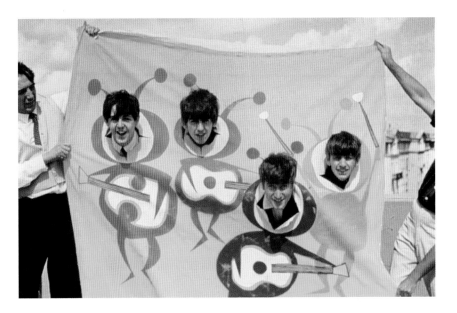

WITH THE BEATLES

The Beatles had five years to prepare for their first album and five months to prepare for their second. After years of meeting up at Paul's house, with hours of spare time on their hands, they were now forced to write in hotel bedrooms, on tour buses and in dressing rooms – anywhere they could snatch a quiet moment.

Such pressures cause some songwriters to dry up, but it proved to be a positive stimulus to John and Paul who, as time went on, developed the ability to write Number 1 hits to order.

John and Paul seemed to have an innate sense of what their public wanted to hear. Believing that it was important for each girl in the audience to feel that they were singing personally to her, many of their songs had the word 'you' in the title – for example, 'From Me To You', 'Thank You Girl', and 'I'll Get You'.

However, if in the early days they'd been able to write for an audience they could see and for people they knew on first-name terms, everything changed once they became successful. Suddenly, the police had to devise ingenious ways of smuggling them in and out of venues, and they were even becoming popular in countries they hadn't visited.

Nonetheless, at the height of Beatlemania, often pursued by scores of screaming fans, they still managed to write a steady stream of successful singles. 'I Want To Hold Your Hand', for example, was written with the American market in mind, and propelled them to the top of the Billboard charts, making them the first British recording artists to truly conquer America. Indeed, constant international travel and the move to London were beneficial for their songwriting as it exposed them to a greater variety of influences. Everybody they met seemed to want to turn them on to something new. Through his relationship with the actress Jane Asher, Paul was becoming more familiar with stage musicals, theatre and classical music. Meanwhile, John was holed up in his Kensington flat listening to imported albums by black American groups like the Miracles, the Shirelles and the Marvelettes.

For *With The Beatles*, the band managed to maintain a steady stream of hit singles despite the distractions of Beatlemania.

With The Beatles, their second album, was a much more considered recording than their first, with sessions spread over a three-month period. It went to Number 1 in Britain shortly after its release in November 1963 and became the first pop album to sell over a million copies. A version of *With The Beatles*, titled *Meet The Beatles*, was released in America in January 1964 and also went to Number 1.

FROM ME TO YOU

'From Me To You', the Beatles' third single, was written on February 28, 1963, while travelling by coach from York to Shrewsbury on the Helen Shapiro tour. Helen can't remember them actually writing it, but can recall it being played to her when they arrived at Shrewsbury in the afternoon ready for their evening concert at the Granada Cinema. "They asked me if I would come and listen to two songs that they had," she says. "Paul sat at the piano and John stood next to me and they sang 'From Me To You' and 'Thank You Girl'. They said they sort of knew their favourite but hadn't finally decided, so they wanted me to tell them which one I thought would make the best A side. As it happened I liked 'From Me To You' and they said, 'Great. That's the one we like.'"

The Beatles played the Odeon Cinema in Southport, Lancashire, the next day, the closest the tour would go to Liverpool, and here they were able to play their new song to Paul's father to get his opinion. They knew the lyrics were simple enough but they were

---

FROM ME TO YOU

Written:	Lennon/McCartney
Length:	1' 57"
UK single release:	April 11, 1963
UK chart position:	1
US single release:	May 27, 1963
US chart position:	41

worried that the music was "a bit on the complicated side" and that "it wouldn't catch on with the fans". It was Paul's dad who convinced them that it was "a nice little tune".

The title was suggested by From You To Us, the letters' column in the *NME*. Paul and John were reading the issue dated February 22, with their tour dates advertised on the front page. They started to "talk about one of the letters in the column", as John revealed in May 1963, when asked about the origins of the song. There were only two letters and it's hard to see which could have provoked comment. One letter complained about 'maniacal laughter' on two recent limbo dance records and the other relished the fact that Cliff Richard appeared to be getting the better of Elvis Presley in the charts. Perhaps it was this last letter that fired the Beatles' own ambition.

Apparently Paul and John started the song by trading lines, making it one of the few Beatle hits that they built from scratch together.

The band donned costumes and visited London's Astoria in Finsbury Park in 1963 for *The Beatles' Christmas Show.*

39

By 1963 Beatlemania was in full swing and the band regularly had to be smuggled in and out of venues to avoid being mobbed by fans.

The song's great gimmick was the use of the high-pitched 'ooooh' sound, inspired by the Isley Brothers' 1962 recording of 'Twist And Shout'. When Kenny Lynch heard them singing this on the coach, he said to them, "You can't do that. You sound like a bunch of fairies", and they replied, "It's okay. The kids will like it." In April 1963, John commented: "We were just fooling about on the guitar. This went on for a while. Then we began to get a good melody line and we really started to work at it. Before the journey was over we'd completed the lyric, everything. We were so pleased..."

A year later, again talking about how the song was written, John said: "Paul and I kicked some ideas around and came up with what we what we thought was a suitable melody line. The words weren't really all that difficult – especially as we had decided quite definitely not to do anything that was at all complicated.

"I suppose that is why we often had the words 'you' and 'me' in the titles of our songs. It's the sort of thing that helps the listeners to identify with the lyrics. We think this is very important. The fans like to feel that they are part of something that is being done by the performers."

From writing to recording took five days although, as John remembered, "We nearly didn't record it because we thought it was too bluesy at first, but when we'd finished it and George Martin had scored it with harmonica, it was all right."

In April 1963 'From Me To You' became the Beatles' second British Number 1 hit but, released on the Vee Jay label in America, it didn't even make the Top 40.

THANK YOU GIRL

Although John and Paul claimed in the early days to have written over 100 songs together between the summer of 1957 and the summer of 1962, Paul admits that the number was closer to 20. Now that they were stars, though, they could no longer afford to be slow in production, as almost everything they wrote from this point on would have to have hit potential. Between 1963 and 1965, they released at least three singles a year and two albums, an incredible output for a group who were touring, filming, meeting the press and writing most of their own material.

At the time the Beatles came into the industry, pop music was formulaic and rather stale. The B sides of singles tended to be throwaway songs, often written by the producer under a pseudonym so that he could reap the benefits of mechanical royalties, and albums contained one or two recent hits plus a lot of filler material. The Beatles changed all this. Suddenly, every song counted. Each of their singles had a B side which was arguably as good as the A side and each album was chock-full of potential singles. Only rarely did their singles appear on albums.

'Thank You Girl', originally titled 'Thank You Little Girl', was written as a follow-up to 'Please Please Me', with 'From Me To You' actually composed as its B side. In the end, it was 'From Me To You' that sounded like the most natural single and so they swapped the two around. At the time, John seemed quite proud of the song but, in 1971, he dismissed it as "just a silly song that we knocked off" and, in 1980, as "one of our efforts at writing a single that didn't work". Paul appears to agree, "A bit of a hack song," he has said, "But all good practice."

THANK YOU GIRL
Written:
Lennon/
McCartney
Length: 2'01"
UK single release:
April 11, 1963 as
B-side of 'From
Me To You'
US single release:
May 27, 1963 as
B-side of 'From
Me To You'

41

SHE LOVES YOU

Although the Beatles had already taken Britain's Number 1 spot twice in 1963, it was 'She Loves You' which took them to the 'toppermost of the poppermost' as they mockingly used to call it. Its sales outstripped anything they'd done before and it went on to be the country's best-selling single of the decade, entering the Top 20 in August 1963 and staying put until February 1964. (In America, it only became a hit after the success of 'I Want To Hold Your Hand'.)

It wasn't simply a commercial triumph. In just over two minutes, the Beatles distilled the essence of everything that made them fresh and exciting. There was the driving beat, the fine harmonizing, the

As hits like 'She Loves You' took the Beatles to the 'toppermost of the poppermost', media interest grew and wacky photocalls became the norm.

SHE LOVES YOU

Written: Lennon/McCartney
Length: 2' 21"
UK single release: August 23, 1963
UK chart position: 1
US single release: September 16, 1963
US chart position: 1

girlish 'wooo' sounds which had gone down so well on 'From Me To You', as well as the bursting enthusiasm of its pace. And on top of this, the distinctive 'Yeah, yeah, yeah' tag which became a gift to headline writers.

The rapid expansion of Beatlemania from regional to national phenomenon can be put down to the Beatles' appearance on *Sunday Night at The London Palladium*, a television show broadcast live from the heart of London on October 13, 1963. Witnessed by a national TV audience of 15 million, screaming fans mobbed the theatre and many of those who packed the streets outside found themselves on the front page of next day's Fleet Street newspapers.

Not only had the Beatles transformed popular music but they had become a phenomenon of post-war Britain. Suddenly they found their photos plastered all over the national papers, not just *Melody Maker*, *New Musical Express* and *Boyfriend*. The single that just happened to be in the centre of this storm was 'She Loves You'.

The song was written by John and Paul in Newcastle after playing the Majestic Ballroom on June 26, 1963. They had a very rare day off before continuing the tour to Leeds on the 28, and Paul remembered being with John at the Turk's Hotel, sitting on separate beds, playing their acoustic guitars.

Their first three singles had been declarations of love with the word 'me' in the title. This time, it was Paul's idea to switch the point of view by making themselves observers of another relationship and addressing the man. Instead of the familiar 'me' and 'you' it became 'she' and 'you'. Paul got the initial idea from Bobby Rydell's then current British hit 'Forget Him' in which the narrator told a girl to forget about a boy who doesn't appear to truly love her.

At first sight, 'She Loves You' is a song about reconciliation. The writer is offering to patch up a broken relationship by passing on messages ('she told me what to say') and offering counsel ('apologize to her').

However, American rock critic Dave Marsh detected 'darker nuances' in the text. In *The Heart Of Rock And Roll*, he wrote: "What Lennon sings boils down to a warning to his friend: You'd better appreciate this woman's friendship, because if you don't, I will." The song remains ambiguous because whether this is really being said as confidential advice to a friend or through gritted teeth to a rival largely depends on how you interpret the tone of voice.

The 'Yeah, yeah, yeah' chorus proved to be a perfect catch phrase for an optimistic era. If Paul's father had had his way, though, things would have been different. On hearing the song for the first time when John and Paul gave it a polish on a quick visit to Forthlin Road, he suggested that they might revise it to 'Yes, yes, yes' because it was more proper. That would have been the Queen's English maybe but not exactly rock'n'roll.

The Beatles were not the first group to use 'yeah yeah'. It was frequently used as an aside in Fifties skiffle music, as well as by Cliff Richard in 'We Say Yeah' (1962) and Elvis Presley in 'All Shook Up' (1957) and 'Good Luck Charm' (1962).

The sixth chord which ends the song was unusual in pop music, although the Glenn Miller Orchestra had used it often on their recordings in the Forties. "George Martin laughed when we first played it to him like that," said Paul. "He thought we were joking. But it didn't work without it so we kept it in and eventually George was convinced."

'She Loves You' was on the surface a positive song of reconciliation, but some critics found an implicit threat in its lyrical leanings.

I'LL GET YOU

'I'll Get You' was written by John and Paul together at John's house as a follow-up to 'From Me To You', and then became the B side of 'She Loves You', a song they wrote days later but which they felt was better. The lyrics, reflective rather than cheerful, appear to owe more to John than Paul and there's a startling similarity between the opening lines ('Imagine I'm in love with you, It's easy 'cos I know') and the opening lines of his 1971 song 'Imagine' ('Imagine there's no heaven, It's easy if you try'). 'I'll Get You' is one of the earliest songs to formulate John's belief in creative visualization – the idea that by imagining changes we want to see, we can actually bring them about. For Paul, who still regards this as one of his favourite Beatles tracks, the use of the word 'imagine' evoked the beginning of a children's fairy tale and offered an invitation into a fictitious world.

One of the song's musical tricks, the shift from D to A minor to break the word 'pretend', was taken from Joan Baez's version of the traditional song 'All My Trials' on her debut album *Joan Baez* (1960). There, the shift takes place in the first line, underneath the words 'don't you cry'.

The Beatles were rapidly becoming more musically sophisticated and 'I'll Get You' saw them stealing a chord change from Sixties icon Joan Baez.

I'LL GET YOU	
Written:	Lennon/McCartney
Length:	2' 04"
UK single release:	August 23, 1963 as B-side of 'She Loves You'
US single release:	September 16, 1963, as B-side of 'She Loves You'

IT WON'T BE LONG

With The Beatles was released in November 1963 as Beatlemania swept Britain. Robert Freeman's black and white cover portraits, where half of each face was in shadow, provided a defining moment in Beatle iconography. Whereas the debut album had been recorded in a day, the sessions for *With The Beatles* were spread over three months, allowing the rawness of a live beat music session to give way to more sophisticated pop production. "That was when we discovered double-tracking," John later commented. "When I

John and Paul's word play on 'be long' and 'belong'' on this early track was aped many years later by George when he came to write 'Blue Jay Way'.

discovered it, I double-tracked everything. I wouldn't let him have anything single-tracked from then on. He (George Martin) would say, 'Please. Just this one,' and I would say, 'No'."

'It Won't Be Long' was the album's opening track, started by John as a potential follow-up single to 'She Loves You', but discarded because, as John said, "it never really made it". Composed as a love song, this could be the story of John's early life. Lonely and rejected, he sits at home waiting for the girl who has walked out on him to come back and make him happy. As in so many later songs, he contrasts the carefree life he imagines everyone else is having with his own anguish, believing that once he's reunited with his loved one all his problems will be solved.

Thelma McGough, who started dating John a month after his mother died in July 1958, believes that his songs of rejection weren't based on broken romances but on the fact that his father had left him as a child and then his mother had effectively left him again by handing him over to her sister to be brought up. "I lost my mother twice," he was to say, "once as a child of five and then again at 17."

"Rejection and betrayal were his experience of life," says Thelma. "When I met him, the first proper conversation we ever had was all about this because my father had done exactly the same thing and so we felt we had something in common. It was that which helped to draw us close. Also, you have to remember that his mother was run down by a car and, although he appeared very controlled about it, you knew that he was hurting inside. We both felt very let down and abandoned. There was a big difference between Paul and John, although as teenagers they'd both lost their mothers. Paul had a very close-knit family with a network of cousins and aunties. His dad was absolutely wonderful. John's life was very isolated. He lived with Mimi (his mother's sister) who looked after him extremely well but there was no closeness. There was nothing tactile about the relationship."

One of the things that excited John and Paul at the time of writing was the word play that they had introduced around the word 'belong'. Although it was a small innovation for them it was to become a hallmark of their more sophisticated writing. Ironically, when George used 'don't be long' in 'Blue Jay Way' four years later Charles Manson thought he was saying 'don't belong' and took it as a message urging him and others to drop out of society.

IT WON'T BE LONG
Written:
Lennon/
McCartney
Length: 2' 13"
UK release:
With The Beatles
album, November 22, 1963
US release:
Meet The Beatles
album, January 20, 1964

49

ALL I'VE GOT TO DO

Half of the 14 songs on *With The Beatles* were written by John and Paul and most of these were written specifically for the album. 'All I've Got To Do', however, was written entirely by John in 1961. The track was, he said, an attempt "to do Smokey Robinson again". His earlier attempt had been with 'Ask Me Why' which was reminiscent of Robinson's 1961 song 'What's So Good About Goodbye'. This time he appears to have used 'You Can Depend On Me' as his model. In 1980, while in the studio recording his vocal track for 'Woman', Yoko commented that John sounded like a Beatle. "Actually, I'm supposed to be Smokey Robinson at the moment, my dear," John answered, "because the Beatles were always supposing that they were Smokey Robinson."

William 'Smokey' Robinson was, in 1963, the 23-year-old leader of the Detroit-based Miracles, a sweet-voiced singer who could also write, arrange and produce songs. Bob Dylan, with perhaps only half of his tongue in his cheek, once referred to him as his favourite living poet. The Beatles also covered his song 'You Really Got A Hold On

ALL I'VE GOT TO DO

Written:	Lennon/McCartney
Length:	2' 04''
UK release:	*With The Beatles* album, November 22, 1963
US release:	*Meet The Beatles* album, January 20, 1964

John composed 'All I've Got To Do' with a very simple motivation in mind: he wanted to write like Motown icon Smokey Robinson.

Me' on this album, which had been a US Top 10 hit for the Miracles in February 1963. "When they recorded that, it was one of the most flattering things that ever happened to me," said Smokey. "I listened to it over and over again, not to criticize it but to enjoy it."

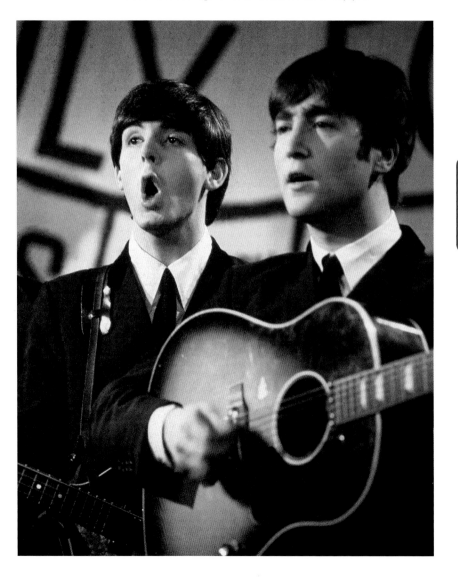

ALL MY LOVING

On April 18, 1963, the actress Jane Asher was in the audience at London's Royal Albert Hall to see the Beatles and other acts in a show which was being recorded by BBC Radio. Although only 17, she was already a successful actress, having appeared in several plays, films and television dramas, besides being a regular guest on BBC Television's pop chart show *Juke Box Jury*. She had been sent to the concert as Britain's 'best-known teenage girl' by the BBC listings magazine *Radio Times*, which wanted to record her comments.

The resulting article, designed to show the effect that the Beatles were having on young people, was published in May 1963, with a photograph of Jane early on in the procedings, looking mature and pensive, contrasted with a later photo of her feigning hysterics. Her comment on the Beatles was: "Now these I could scream for". Little did she know at the time that she would become the best-known of all Paul McCartney's girlfriends and would inspire some of his greatest love songs. She met up with the group after the show at the Royal Court Hotel in Chelsea and it wasn't long before she and Paul became locked in conversation. Shortly afterwards they began dating and, before the end of 1963, Paul had moved into a room at the Ashers' home at 57 Wimpole Street in London's West End.

It was a significant change for Paul because, within a year of leaving his council house in Allerton, he was living in one of the most expensive areas of London's West End with a family which had a number of important social connections. Jane's father was a medical consultant and her mother a professor at the Guildhall School of Music. They had a study filled with paintings and scattered with scientific journals, where talk could range from pop music and theatre to some new

ALL MY LOVING
Written:
Lennon/
McCartney
Length: 2' 09"
UK release:
With The Beatles
album, November
22, 1963
US release:
Meet The Beatles
album, January 20,
1964

The Beatles appeared on BBC pop show *Juke Box Jury*, presented by the suave David Jacobs.

development in psychology. It all helped to broaden Paul's horizons and this in turn would affect his songwriting.

'All My Loving' was conceived as a poem by Paul one day as he was shaving. It wasn't until he'd finished his day's work that he put music to it, initially imagining it as a country and western song as he worked on the tune backstage at a British theatre while on tour. "It was the first song I ever wrote where I had the words before the music," he said. Like so many Beatle songs now that they were almost permanently on tour, it was about being separated, but whereas John would have been filled with apprehension, Paul is confident that things will work out. John, who was often grudging in his praise for Paul's songs, called it "a damn good piece of work".

LITTLE CHILD

As the lyrics to 'Little Child' are about a 'sad and lonely' boy wanting a girl to take a chance on him, the initial idea probably came from John. Asked about 'Little Child' in 1980, all John would say was that it was another effort to write a song for somebody, "probably Ringo". Paul later remembered that part of the song's melody was inspired by 'Whistle My Love', a 1950s song recorded by the British folk singer Elton Hayes and used in the Walt Disney film *Robin Hood*.

The earliest extant draft of the lyric is in Paul's hand and is substantially the same as the later record with the exception of the opening line to the first verse. On the record it is, 'Now if you want someone to make you feel so fine' but it was originally, 'If you want someone to have a ravin' time'.

The Beatles were now entering a period where they were being asked to provide songs for other artists. In April 1963, John had gone on holiday to Spain with Brian Epstein who used the opportunity to try to persuade him to write original material for the other acts he managed. The Beatles duly complied, writing 'I'll Be On My Way' and 'Bad To Me' for Billy J Kramer and the Dakotas, 'Tip Of My Tongue' for Tommy Quickly, 'Love Of The Loved' for Cilla Black, and 'Hello Little Girl' for the Fourmost.

Paul has since admitted they "knocked them out" in the belief that it was the job of a songwriting team to keep writing songs, reserving the best ones for themselves and giving the rest away.

Despite being a fairly melancholic song, 'Little Child' was probably written with the band's joker, Ringo, in mind.

LITTLE CHILD
Written:
Lennon/
McCartney
Length: 1' 48"
UK release:
With The Beatles
album, November 22, 1963
US release:
Meet The Beatles
album, January 20, 1964

DON'T BOTHER ME

'Don't Bother Me' was the first song by George Harrison ever to be recorded by the Beatles and indeed the first lyrical composition that he had ever come up with. He wrote it in August 1963 while staying at the Palace Court Hotel in Bournemouth. The Beatles were playing six nights at the seaside town's Gaumont Cinema and it was during this week that the photographer Robert Freeman came down to take the celebrated album cover photographs.

"I wrote the song as an exercise to see if I could write a song," George said. "I was sick in bed. Maybe that's why it turned out to be 'Don't Bother Me'." Bill Harry, the founder of the Liverpool music paper *Mersey Beat*, has suggested the title had another origin. Apparently, Harry used to pester George whenever he saw him to find out if he'd written anything since his first instrumental composition 'Cry For A Shadow' which was included on an album by Tony Sheridan in 1962. "When George was about to go out one night, he thought he might bump into me," Harry wrote, "so he started writing a number which he called 'Don't Bother Me'."

DON'T BOTHER ME

Written:	Harrison
Length:	2' 29"
UK release:	*With The Beatles* album, November 22, 1963
US release:	*Meet The Beatles* album, January 20, 1964

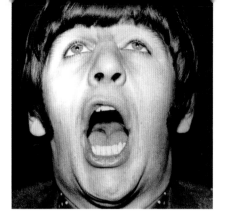

HOLD ME TIGHT

A version of 'Hold Me Tight' was recorded for the Beatles' first album but not used and rather than go back to the old tape they re-cut it for *With The Beatles*. Written by Paul, who considered it a "work song", John's only comment was that he "was never really interested in it either way".

It was influenced by the Shirelles, the New Jersey group who in 1961 had become the first all-girl group to make the Number 1 spot in the American charts. The Beatles were consistent champions of girl groups and girl singers, citing acts such as the Chiffons, Mary Wells, the Ronettes, the Donays and the Crystals as influences on their close harmony vocals. Even before they arrived in London, they were including Shirelles' songs in their act and on their debut album they featured two of them – 'Baby It's You' and 'Boys'.

The Shirelles – Shirley Owens, Micki Harris, Doris Coley and Beverly Lee – had seven Top 20 hits in America and three in Britain but 1963 proved to be their last year of chart glory as they were pushed aside by the invasion of British beat.

Although to most listeners at the time it sounded like a song about a quick 'kiss and cuddle' it was about a full sexual encounter. The narrator is alone with the girl at night and 'making love'.

Most pop songs at the time tended not to be so bold. The original lyric sheet, complete with doodles of a man's head, was reproduced in Mike McCartney's book *Thank U Very Much* (1981).

Ringo-sung songs such as 'I Wanna Be Your Man' (right) functioned as light relief.

HOLD ME TIGHT
Written:
Lennon/
McCartney
Length: 2' 32"
UK release:
With The Beatles
album, November
22, 1963
US release:
Meet The Beatles
album, January 20,
1964

I WANNA BE YOUR MAN

Although Ringo didn't have much of a singing voice he sang one number in each show that was within his limited vocal range and this tradition was carried on with the albums, with a doleful Ringo spot slotted in almost as light relief. It was with Ringo in mind that Paul started writing 'I Wanna Be Your Man', a basic four-chord number the lyric of which didn't progress much beyond the five words in the title but the song has become best known for the version recorded by the Rolling Stones.

The Beatles had known the group's manager Andrew Oldham since they first arrived in London because Brian Epstein had briefly hired him as the group's publicist. In April 1963, he had been tipped off about the Rolling Stones who were playing at the Station Hotel in Richmond. Soon afterwards he became their manager. He was a born hustler who created the Stones' bad boy image by getting the group to look mean when photographed, playing up any signs of anti-social behaviour and suggesting controversial headlines to newspapers and magazines.

Five months after taking the Stones on, he was anxious to find them good material for singles. Mick Jagger and Keith Richard were not yet writing and the group's first single, which had sold 100,000 copies, had been a cover of the Chuck Berry song 'Come On'.

On September 10th 1963 when John and Paul were leaving the Charing Cross Road offices of their publisher Dick James they bumped into Oldham in the street. He shared this concern about finding new material with the two Beatles who had already seen the Stones perform twice in London clubs and Paul immediately mentioned 'I Wanna Be Your Man'. They all then walked along to

I WANNA BE YOUR MAN
Written:
Lennon/
McCartney
Length: 1' 58"
UK release:
With The Beatles
album, November
22, 1963
US release:
Meet The Beatles
album, January 20,
1964

57

Studio 51 in Great Newport Street, a club run by jazz man Ken Colyer, where the Stones were rehearsing.

The song was played to the group and Brian Jones, then their acknowledged leader, said that he liked it and Decca was pressurizing them for a single. John and Paul talked it over and then John said, "Listen, if you guys really like the main part of the song, we'll finish it for you right now." They went off to a separate room and a few minutes later emerged with the completed song.

It was meant to emulate the feel of the Shirelles' song 'Boys' which Ringo sang in concert. It was the sound of the song rather than the lyrics that mattered for him. The dragged out 'maaaan' of the chorus was inspired by Benny Spellman's song 'Fortune Teller', the B side to his 1962 hit 'Lipstick Traces'.

'I Wanna Be Your Man', which the Stones recorded on October 7th 1963, went to Number 12 in Britain and helped to turn the group into a major act. The press liked to portray the Beatles and the Stones as the deadliest of enemies but in fact they were always close friends, turning up at each other's sessions and socializing in clubs. John later commented that, as far as the Beatles were concerned, 'I Wanna Be Your Man' was a 'throwaway' song, which is why they were happy to give it away before they had even recorded it themselves (which they did the next day with Ringo as vocalist). "We weren't going to give them anything great, right?" John said.

Prince Philip presents the band with a single award at the Carl-Alan Awards in the Empire Ballroom, Leicester Square, in March 1964.

NOT A SECOND TIME

Paul has said that the musical inspiration behind 'Not A Second Time' was again Smokey Robinson and the Miracles, whereas the main writing honours were claimed by John. It was another example of John allowing his feelings, in this case of being wounded, to wash all over his work. After having been let down and made to cry the writer's response is to shut down his emotions because he can't face the possibility of being hurt all over again.

It was one of the first of the Beatles' songs to be subjected to critical analysis by a quality newspaper. William Mann, then music critic of the *Times* (London), compared part of it to Gustav Mahler's 'Song Of The Earth'. John would later say that this review was responsible for "starting the whole intellectual bit about the Beatles".

"Harmonic interest is typical of their quicker songs too," Mann wrote, "and one gets the impression that they think simultaneously of harmony and melody, so firmly are the major tonic sevenths and ninths built into their tunes, and the flat-submediant key-switches, so natural is the Aeolian cadence at the end of 'Not A Second Time'" John's comment on this was, "I didn't know what the hell it was all about". Another time he said that he thought Aeolian cadences sounded like exotic birds. He wasn't the only one to be confused by Mann's terminology. An 'Aeolian cadence' is not a recognised musical description and generations of music critics have puzzled over exactly what Mann was referring to. The review itself however has been credited with initiating serious musical criticism of the Beatles' work.

NOT A SECOND
TIME
Written:
Lennon/
McCartney
Length: 2' 08"
UK release:
With The Beatles
album, November
22, 1963
US release:
Meet The Beatles
album, January 20,
1964

I WANT TO HOLD YOUR HAND

There was a piano in the basement den of the Ashers' home in Wimpole Street where John and Paul would sometimes work. It was here on October 16th 1963 that they created 'I Want To Hold Your Hand', the song that was to finally break them in America when it reached the Number 1 spot in January 1964.

It was a remarkable achievement because no British pop artists had ever really cracked America. In 1956 Lonnie Donegan, the 'king of skiffle', had reached the Top 10 with 'Rock Island Line' but only after four months of touring. Cliff Richard had toured, released a movie and appeared on the *Ed Sullivan Show* but had only a minor hit with 'Living Doll'. The only British records ever to make the Number 1 position had been Vera Lynn with 'Auf Wiedersehen' in 1952, Acker Bilk with 'Stranger On The Shore' in 1961 and the Tornadoes with 'Telstar' in 1962. After disappointing sales on the Vee

I WANT TO HOLD YOUR HAND

Written: Lennon/McCartney
Length: 2' 24"
UK single release: November 29, 1963
UK chart position: 1
US single release: December 26, 1963
US chart position: 1

The Beatles wrote 'I Want To Hold Your Hand' with 'an American sound in mind' and it broke them in the US.

Jay and Swan labels, the Beatles were now with Capitol in America and Brian Epstein had promised that the first single for them would be designed with an 'American sound' in mind.

According to John, 'I Want To Hold Your Hand' sprang into being when, having come up with an opening line, Paul hit a chord on the piano. "I turned to him and said, 'That's it! Do that again!' In those days, we really used to absolutely write like that – both playing into each other's noses." Gordon Waller, schoolboy friend of Jane Asher's older brother Peter (with whom he had formed the singing duo Peter and Gordon), was also in the house that day. "As far as I can remember John was on a pedal organ and Paul was on a piano," he said. "The basement was the place where we all went to make our 'noise' and they called us down to hear this song they'd just written. It wasn't totally complete but the structure and the chorus were there."

The Beatles were, of course, still playing to their market, the teenage girls for whom hand holding and kissing was the ultimate in physical expression. 'I Want To Hold Your Hand' certainly wasn't an indication of their own sexual reticence.

Robert Freeman, the photographer who took the cover photo for *With The Beatles*, lived in a flat beneath John at 13 Emperor's

'This Boy' (right) saw the band mimicking the close harmonies of the Everly Brothers.

Gate in Kensington and tried to educate him in jazz and experimental music while John directed him towards rock'n'roll. "He (John) was intrigued by a contemporary French album of experimental music," Freeman recalled. "There was one track where a musical phrase repeated, as if the record had stuck. This effect was used in 'I Want To Hold Your Hand' – at my suggestion – 'that my love, I can't hide, I can't hide, I can't hide'."

The Beatles heard that 'I Want To Hold Your Hand' had made it to Number 1 in America when they were playing in Paris and it triggered plans for their first Stateside visit. It was because they knew that Cliff Richard had failed to set the charts alight there, despite having toured, that they determined only to make appearances when they could warrant top billing.

THIS BOY

'This Boy' was written by John and Paul in a hotel bedroom as an exercise in three-part harmony, which they had never attempted on record before, and was inspired, as so much else was at the time, by Smokey Robinson and the Miracles. "The middle eight," said George, "was John trying to do Smokey."

The lyrics, John said, amounted to nothing. All that was important was "sound and harmony". Harmony was integral to the early Beatles' work, and the influence of the Everly Brothers in particular is evident in this song. They'd become familiar with three-part harmonizing by singing Phil Spector's 'To Know Him Is To Love Him', a 1959 hit for the Teddy Bears.

Saying that the lyrics amounted to nothing was not the same as saying that they were without meaning, for again John was portraying himself here as a loser waiting for his loved one to return.

THIS BOY
Written: Lennon/McCartney
Length: 2' 12"
UK single release: November 29, 1963 as B-side of 'I Want To Hold Your Hand'
US release: *Meet The Beatles* album, January 20, 1964

I CALL YOUR NAME

John reckoned that he wrote 'I Call Your Name' back when "there was no Beatles and no group". As the Quarry Men, his first group, was formed very shortly after the acquisition of his first guitar in March 1957, he must have either written it as he was learning to play

I CALL YOUR NAME

Written:	Lennon/McCartney
Length:	2' 09"
UK release:	On 'Long Tall Sally' EP, June 19, 1964
US release:	*The Beatles' Second Album*, April 10, 1964

or even earlier when he could only play banjo, although Paul can remember working on it in John's bedroom at Menlove Avenue. The Quarry Men was initially a skiffle group made up of friends from Quarry Bank High School for Boys. Rod Davis, who played banjo with them, can't recall John writing songs in those days. "What we did was to listen to the latest singles when they were played on the radio and try to copy the words down," he says. "The trouble was, if you couldn't make them out, or couldn't write quickly enough, you were stuck. So what John used to do was to add his own words to these tunes. No one ever seemed to notice because they didn't know the words either. There was a song called 'Streamline Train' which John rewrote as 'Long Black Train'. He also put new words to the Del Vikings' hit 'Come Go With Me' and I didn't realize what he'd done until I heard the original version many years later."

If the song was written as long ago as John thought, it's interesting that even in his schooldays he was writing about despair. The lines 'I never weep at night, I call your name' are close to his 1971 lines 'In the middle of the night, I call your name' in 'Oh Yoko' on the *Imagine* album.

John added the Jamaican blue beat instrumental break in 1964. Blue beat and ska music, brought to Britain by immigrants from the West Indies, were becoming popular with British mods and the Blue Beat label, founded by Ziggy Jackson in 1961, had released 213 singles in the previous three years. Two weeks after the recording of 'I Call Your Name', the *New Musical Express* asked whether ska and blue beat were going to be the major new talking point in pop music. With the Beatles around, there was no chance of that.

John had only just graduated from the banjo to guitar when he wrote 'I Call Your Name' in the Fifties.

A HARD DAY'S NIGHT

A Hard Day's Night marked a breakthrough as it was the first of their albums where every track was written by the Beatles. It was also a personal *tour de force* for John, who was the major contributor to ten of the album's 13 tracks. Being the oldest in the group and the founder member of the Quarry Men, John was the unacknowledged leader in those days. Although Paul was more musically accomplished – he had mastered guitar and piano ahead of John – they still maintained the same junior to senior pupil relationship established when they met in 1957.

John later recognized that this was his dominant period in the Beatles and it was only when, in his own words, he became "self-conscious and inhibited" that Paul began to take over. The majority of the group's singles up to this point, John claimed, had either been written by him, or featured him as lead vocalist. The only reason Paul sang on the track of 'A Hard Day's Night' was because John couldn't reach the high notes.

Seven of the songs were written for *A Hard Day's Night* although one of these, 'I'll Cry Instead', was eventually dropped in favour of 'Can't Buy Me Love', a single which Paul had written under pressure. The Beatles were still writing pop songs to deadlines but putting more of their personal concerns into the lyrics. For example, 'If I Fell' revealed a lot about John's troubled psyche. Equally, 'And I Love Her' was one of Paul's most personal songs yet – a declaration of his feelings for Jane Asher. At the time, few people knew how or why the songs had been written. It wouldn't be until the Beatles broke up that the authorship of individual songs became widely known and details, such as those behind the breakdown of John and Cynthia's marriage, would be revealed.

This one will sleigh you: the band pile on top of a sledge for the shooting of the *A Hard Day's Night* film.

Initially, the film of *A Hard Day's Night* was conceived as a vehicle to sell an album but, as with everything the Beatles touched in 1964, it turned into a great commercial success, recouping its production costs almost 30 times over. The initial premise was to capture the delirium of Beatlemania, in the style of a black and white television documentary. Designed to display their musical rather than acting abilities the Beatles were given undemanding acting roles with short lines and a strong supporting cast of character actors to cover any weaknesses.

"I was with the Beatles in Paris when they played there in January 1964," says screenwriter Alun Owen. "I was also around them in an unofficial capacity on a lot of other occasions. The biggest nonsense that has been written about the film is that it was ad-libbed. It wasn't. At the time they were 22 or 23 years old. They had never acted before. If you go through the script, you'll see that no sentence is longer than six words, because they couldn't have handled any more. The only ad-libs were made by John."

The Beatles were pleased with the final result. Although they knew it only showed one side of their personalities and wasn't as realistic as it could have been, they recognized that *A Hard Day's Night* avoided the clichés of most pop movies.

The album was released in America in June 1964 and a month later in Britain, making the Number 1 spot in both countries. The American version was substantially different, featuring only the seven soundtrack songs and 'I'll Cry Instead'. It was made up to a 12-track album by including several of George Martin's orchestral versions of Lennon and McCartney's songs.

A HARD DAY'S NIGHT

In the early Sixties, it was customary for pop stars to make a movie after a decent string of hits, just as Elvis Presley had done in the Fifties. The assumption was that movie stardom was longer lasting and more substantial than pop stardom. The *Young Ones* (1961) and *Summer Holiday* (1962) were big box-office hits in the UK for Cliff Richard, and even lesser British names such as Adam Faith, Tommy Steele, Billy Fury and Terry Dene had made it on to the silver screen.

The Beatles wanted to do something from a different angle and were fortunate in being introduced to director Dick Lester, whose fast cuts and imaginative camera work perfectly suited the excitement and freshness of pop. Negotiations over the film had begun in October 1963 and, in November, Liverpool-born writer Alun Owen, who had an ear for the Beatles' natural speech patterns, accompanied the group to Dublin and Belfast to observe them at work and catch the flavour of Beatlemania.

The Beatles had to write the songs for the film without having seen Owen's screenplay. Three were written in Paris during January 1964, three the next month in Miami during one two-hour session and the title track back home in in London. "All of the songs, except for 'A Hard Day's Night', were written independently of what I was writing," says Alun Owen. "Paul and John wrote them and they were woven into the script as things came up. None of them bear any relation to the story. They were just numbers."

The Beatles didn't have a title for the film, having already rejected *On The Move*, *Let's Go* and *Beatlemania*. 'A Hard Day's Night' was the last song written and it eventually became the title to both the album and the film. The phrase was attributed to Ringo Starr, who

The band have their moptops tended by Pattie Boyd, Tina Williams, Pru Berry and Susan Whiteman.

said in 1964: "I came up with the phrase 'a hard day's night'. It just came out. We went to do a job and we worked all day and then we happened to work all night. I came out, still thinking it was day and said, 'It's been a hard day…looked around, saw that it was dark and added…'s night.'"

If Ringo did invent the phrase it must have been in 1963, and not on the set of the film as has been reported, because John included it in his book *In His Own Write* which was written that year. In the story 'Sad Michael' John had the line, "He'd had a hard days [sic] night that day…" However it came about, Dick Lester liked it as a title because it summed up the frenetic pace of the film as well as the humour of the Beatles and, as he was driving him home one night, he told John that he planned to use it. The next morning John brought along a song to go with it.

The *Evening Standard* journalist Maureen Cleave, who had been one of the first London journalists to write about the Beatles

A HARD DAY'S NIGHT

Written: Lennon/McCartney

Length: 2' 32"

UK single release: July 10, 1964

UK chart position: 1

US release: *A Hard Day's Night* album, June 26, 1964

(*Evening Standard,* February 2, 1963), can recall John coming into the studio on April 16, 1964, with the lyrics written on the back of a card to his son Julian, who had just had his first birthday. Initially the song ran: 'But when I get home to you, I find my tiredness is through, And I feel all right'. Cleave told him that she thought 'my tiredness is through' was a weak line. John took out a pen, crossed through the line, and wrote; 'I find the things that you do, They make me feel all right'. Maureen said that "The song seemed to materialize as if by magic. It consisted of John humming to the others, then they would all put their heads together and hum and three hours later they had this record."

Although Paul hadn't written the lyric, when promoting the film in America, he was asked to explain how it was put together. "It seemed a bit ridiculous writing a song called 'A Hard Day's Night'," he said, "because it sounded a funny phrase at the time but the idea came of saying that it had been a hard day's night and we'd been working all day and you get back to a girl and everything's fine. So it was turned into one of those songs."

'A Hard Day's Night' was featured over the opening and closing credits of the film. It was the first cut on the soundtrack album and became a Number 1 single in Britain and America. The comic actor Peter Sellers, once a member of John's favourite radio comedy group the Goons, recorded 'A Hard Day's Night' by speaking the lyric as if he was Laurence Olivier delivering a Shakespearean monologue. It made the British Top 20 in December 1965.

I SHOULD HAVE KNOWN BETTER

I SHOULD HAVE KNOWN BETTER
Written:
Lennon/
McCartney
Length: 2' 44"
UK release:
A Hard Day's Night album, July 10, 1964
US release:
A Hard Day's Night album, June 26, 1964

Released as the flip side of 'A Hard Day's Night' in America, 'I Should Have Known Better' was the first song in the film and was performed in a sequence where the Beatles and Paul's 'grandfather' (played by Wilfred Brambell) are on a train and banished to the mail van. They start playing cards and, several cuts later, appear with guitars, harmonica and drums. "It just seemed the natural place to have the first number," says Alun Owen.

Although much of the filming took place on trains travelling between London and the West Country, 'I Should Have Known Better' was actually filmed on a set at Twickenham Film Studios.

Surprisingly for a song by John it is very optimistic: he loves her, she loves him and everything is fine.

The Beatles sang 'I Should Have Known Better' in *A Hard Day's Night* as they emerged from a train's mail van.

IF I FELL

In *A Hard Day's Night* John had to sing 'If I Fell' to Ringo because there was no obvious place for it in the already-written script and no love interest. "We're in the television studio and Ringo is supposed to be sulking a bit," Paul explained in 1964. "John starts joking with him and then sings the song as though we're singing it to him. We got fits of the giggles just doing it."

The recording started on February 27, 1964 and, as the earliest draft of the song was written on a Valentine's Day card, it can be assumed that it was written somewhere in the two weeks between February 14 and 27.

'If I Fell' is one of John's most beautiful songs and is about an illicit relationship. He is asking the woman in question for an assurance that if he leaves his wife for her that she'll love him more than he's ever been loved. It is about someone eager to avoid confrontation.

In the early draft he had written 'I hope that she will cry/ When she hears we are two' rather than the final, softer 'And that she will cry…' This suggests that his first thought was a cruel sense of pleasure from his partner discovering his unfaithfulness. The cruelty is still there but it's harder to detect.

John said that the song was 'semi-autobiographical' and it is known that he was unfaithful to his wife Cynthia although she was oblivious to what was going on. "I'm a coward," he later said in 1968. "I wasn't going to go off and leave Cynthia and be by myself."

John saw this as his first proper ballad and a precursor to 'In My Life', his song about growing up, which was to use the same chord sequence.

John' had to use 'If I Fell, one of his most beautiful love songs, to serenade.Ringo.

IF I FELL
Written:
Lennon/
McCartney
Length: 2' 22"
UK release:
A Hard Day's Night album,
July 10, 1964
US release:
A Hard Day's Night album,
June 26, 1964

AND I LOVE HER

Paul's love of rock'n'roll didn't mean that he despised the popular music that had preceded it. He loved the big band music of the Twenties and Thirties which his father played, the Victorian music-hall songs which his relatives sang round the piano and the show tunes of the Forties and Fifties.

Even in the days of Hamburg and the Cavern Club in Liverpool, Paul had sung 'Till There Was You', a song from the 1957 Broadway musical *The Music Man*, later popularized by Peggy Lee, and this was included on *With The Beatles*. Its success must have made him realize that ballads enriched the show, and wrote 'And I Love Her' to fill this space. John said it was Paul's first 'Yesterday'. Paul said it was, "the first song that I impressed myself with".

The initial idea was to write a song with a title that began mid-sentence. Paul then wrote the verses and came to John for help with the middle eight. It didn't escape Paul's notice that almost a decade later Perry Como recorded a song titled 'And I Love You So'.

Recording on the song began in February 1964 and it was the first Beatle track to feature just acoustic instruments (Ringo played bongos). In the film *A Hard Day's Night,* they are shown recording it for a television show.

Only the month before recording, Jane Asher commented to American writer Michael Braun: "The trouble (with Paul) is that he wants the fans' adulation and mine too. He's so selfish. That's his biggest fault. He can't see that my feelings for him are real and that the fans' (feelings for him) are fantasy." Paul has since said that it wasn't written with anyone in mind but it's hard to believe that in his first flush of love with Jane Asher he was writing such tender songs to an imaginary girl.

AND I LOVE HER
Written:
Lennon/
McCartney
Length: 2' 31"
UK release:
A Hard Day's Night album,
July 10, 1964
US release:
A Hard Day's Night album,
June 26, 1964

73

I'M HAPPY JUST TO DANCE WITH YOU

John and Paul wrote 'I'm Happy Just To Dance With You' for George to sing in the film "to give him a piece of the action" and it was filmed on stage at the Scala Theatre in Charlotte Street, London. As the youngest member of the Beatles, George was living in the shadow of Paul and John. When he started writing his own songs, he was resentful that more of them weren't considered for the albums.

John was equally hurt in 1980 when George published his biography *I Me Mine* and made no mention of John's influence on his songwriting. Paul has admitted that 'I'm Happy Just To Dance With You' was a 'formula song'.

I'M HAPPY JUST TO DANCE WITH YOU
Written: Lennon/ McCartney
Length: 1' 58"
UK release: *A Hard Day's Night* album, July 10, 1964
US release: *A Hard Day's Night* album, June 26, 1964

George opens fan mail as he celebrates his 21st birthday, on February 25, 1964, with the help of a Beatles' management company employee.

TELL ME WHY

'Tell Me Why' was written to provide an 'upbeat' number for the concert sequence in *A Hard Day's Night*. John thought of something the Chiffons or the Shirelles might do and "knocked it off".

It's a typical John scenario. He has been lied to and deserted. He's crying. He appeals to his girl to let him know what he's done wrong so that he can put it right. Children whose parents either leave them or die suddenly are often left with a feeling that they must in some way be responsible. 'If there's something I have said or done, Tell me what and I'll apologize', John sang.

It was only when he underwent primal therapy in 1970 that he came to terms with these subconscious fears. Therapist Arthur Janov set him the exercise of looking back through all his Beatles' songs to see what they revealed of his anxieties. On his first post-therapy album, *John Lennon/Plastic Ono Band*, he was able to sing about these traumas in their original context in songs such as 'Mother', 'Hold On', 'Isolation' and 'My Mummy's Dead'.

TELL ME WHY	
Written:	Lennon/McCartney
Length:	2' 10"
UK release:	*A Hard Day's Night* album, July 10, 1964
US release:	*A Hard Day's Night* album, June 26, 1964

CAN'T BUY ME LOVE

In January 1964, the Beatles went to Paris for 18 days of concerts at the Olympia Theatre. They stayed at the five-star George V hotel, just off the Champs Élysées, and an upright piano was moved into one of their suites so that songwriting could continue. It was here that John and Paul wrote 'One And One Is Two' for fellow Liverpool group the Strangers and Paul came up with 'Can't Buy Me Love'.

With a new single due in March and the news that 'I Want To Hold Your Hand' had rocketed to the top of the American charts, there was no time to waste. George Martin, who had come to the Pathé Marconi Studios in Paris to record the newly-written song along with German language versions of 'She Loves You' ('Sie Liebt Dich') and 'I Want To Hold Your Hand' ('Komm, Gib Mir Deine Hand'), made the suggestion of starting it with the chorus. Although 'She Loves You', 'I Wanna Be Your Man', 'Don't Bother Me' and 'All My Loving' were all used in *A Hard Day's Night*, 'Can't Buy Me Love' was the only previously-released song to be included on the soundtrack album. This was because it was pulled into the film at a late stage to replace 'I'll Cry Instead', which director Dick Lester didn't think was right for the scene where the Beatles break out.

'Can't Buy Me Love' was used in the film as the group ran down a fire escape at the back of the theatre (actually the Odeon in Hammersmith, London) and fooled around on some open ground (playing fields in Isleworth). It was the group's first experience of freedom in the film after having been locked for days in cars, trains, dressing rooms and hotels. Screenwriter Alun Owen remembers: "My stage direction at this point was very simple. It read: 'The boys come down the fire escape. It is the first time they have been free. They run about and play silly buggers'."

CAN'T BUY
ME LOVE
Written:
Lennon/
McCartney
Length: 2' 14"
UK single release:
March 20, 1964
**UK chart
position:** 1
US single release:
March 16, 1964
**US chart
position:** 1

Paul examines his own waxwork at Madame Tussaud's in London in April 1964.

The lyric suggests it's partly an answer song to Berry Gordy and Janie Bradford's 'Money', a number the Beatles had started performing in 1960 and had recorded on *With The Beatles*. The Gordy/Bradford line was that money could get you anything. The Lennon/McCartney response was that it could get you anything but love. Paul has cited Little Richard as a musical influence and Dominic Pedler (*The Beatles as Musicians*) suggests that it was 'Lucille' that supplied the template for the verses.

American journalists asked Paul in 1966 whether 'Can't Buy Me Love' was a song about prostitution. He replied that all the songs were open to interpretation but that that particular suggestion was taking things too far.

ANY TIME AT ALL

Having written the songs which would be used in the film, the race was on to come up with a number for what would be the second side of the soundtrack album.

John was obviously the more prolific songwriter at the time, having written five of the seven songs in the film and going on to write all but one of the tracks on the other side. This had not been achieved without some difficulty. 'Any Time At All', he later admitted, was a rewriting of his earlier song 'It Won't Be Long', using the same chord progression from C to A minor and back and, when it came to recording, employing the same bawling vocal style.

His original draft of the song was two verses longer, the third verse starting; 'I'll be waiting here all alone/ Just like I've always done…' but there were already enough words in the song and neither of the additional verses advanced the story.

In January 1964 he spoke about some of the changes in his songwriting techniques. "If I found a new chord (I used to) write a song around it," he said. "I thought that if there were a million chords I'd never run out. Sometimes the chords got to be an obsession and we started to put unnecessary ones in. We then decided to keep the songs simple and it's the best way. It might have sounded okay for us but the extra chords wouldn't make other people like them any better. That's the way we've kept it all along."

There were only three other occasions when he claimed Beatles' songs had been recycled. 'Yes It Is' he said was a rewrite of 'This Boy', 'Paperback Writer' was "Son of 'Day Tripper'" and 'Get Back' was a "potboiler rewrite" of 'Lady Madonna'.

Despite the Beatles' stellar productivity, John confessed that the band occasionally recycled song ideas.

ANY TIME AT ALL
Written:
Lennon/
McCartney
Length: 2' 13"
UK release:
A Hard Day's Night
album, July 10,
1964
US release:
Something New
album, July 20,
1964

I'LL CRY INSTEAD

I'll Cry Instead' was the song originally set to be used over the fire escape sequence in *A Hard Day's Night* but then dropped in favour of the already-released 'Can't Buy Me Love'. However, when the film was re-mastered for video release in 1986, the song was put back in by running it over a collage sequence preceding the opening credits.

John had written about crying in many of his songs to date but 'I'll Cry Instead' was different in that he was saying that once he'd finished crying he would return to seek vengeance. He imagined coming back and breaking girls' hearts around the world, as if by causing people to fall for him and then spurning them, he would be able to punish everyone who had ever rejected him. He would later admit having been violent at times and in 'Getting Better' he was able to write about his cruelty to women as something he had overcome.

This was also the first song in which John admitted having a chip on his shoulder, a sign that he was entering a period of intense self-examination, that was to continue until his first solo albums, after the break-up of the Beatles.

I'LL CRY INSTEAD

Written:	Lennon/McCartney
Length:	1' 47"
UK release:	*A Hard Day's Night* album, July 10, 1964
US release:	*A Hard Day's Night* album, June 26, 1964

THINGS WE SAID TODAY

In May 1964, having completed the filming of *A Hard Day's Night* and after fulfilling some performing commitments in England and Scotland, the Beatles and their partners took off for a holiday break. John and George made a round-the-world trip with stop-offs in Holland, Polynesia, Hawaii and Canada, while Paul and Ringo went to France and Portugal before taking off for the Virgin Islands.

Ringo turned 24 on July 7, 1964, and the next day the Beatles obligingly gave him the bumps at a BBC studio.

While in the Caribbean, Paul hired a yacht called *Happy Days* and it was while on board with Ringo, Maureen and Jane that he wrote 'Things We Said Today' on his acoustic guitar. He started the song in one of the cabins but found the smell of engine oil too nauseating so he came up and finished sitting out on the back deck.

The song was a reflection on his relationship with Jane in light of the fact that he knew, by the nature of their work, that times together would be few. When they were separated, he said, he would take comfort from the memory of the things they'd said that day.

THINGS WE SAID TODAY

Written: Lennon/McCartney
Length: 2' 38"
UK single release: July 10, 1964 as B-side of 'A Hard Day's Night'
US release: *Something New* album, July 20, 1964

WHEN I GET HOME

Too innovative to be satisfied with a mere guitar/bass/drums set-up, the Beatles made frequent use of more exotic instrumentation.

'When I Get Home' was described by John as a "four-in-the-bar cowbell song", influenced by his love of Motown and American soul music. Around the time it was recorded, he was asked what song he wished he had written and he said his first choice would be Marvin Gaye's 'Can I Get A Witness'. "Then there's other stuff on Tamla Motown that we like," he went on. "It's harder to write good 12-bar numbers because so much has been done before with them. I'd rather write a song with chords all over the place."

An unusually optimistic song for John, the lyric revealed his thoughts about what he was going to say and do to his 'girl', when he got home. Slightly close in subject matter to the single 'A Hard Day's Night' ('when I get home to you...') it shows that he still thought of home as the place where true love would be waiting. Despite his image as the 'lad' in the group, John was really a 'homebody' who liked nothing more than to curl up in front of a television with a supply of books and magazines. It's fitting that he spent much of his final decade as a 'house husband', happy to be confined to his rooms in the Dakota Buildings in New York.

83

WHEN I GET HOME

Written:	Lennon/McCartney
Length:	2' 18"
UK release:	*A Hard Day's Night* album, July 10, 1964
US release:	*Something New* album, July 20, 1964

YOU CAN'T
DO THAT

In both Britain and America 'You Can't Do That' became the B side of 'Can't Buy Me Love'. In this song, instead of weeping, John tries threatening. He tells his girl that if he catches her talking to another boy he's going to leave her immediately. He knows what it feels like to be spurned and he's determined that it won't happen again.

The musical influence, John later said, was Wilson Pickett, the former gospel singer from Alabama who at the time had only released three singles under his own name in America, only one of which had been a minor hit. It wasn't until 1965, his contract then having been acquired by Atlantic Records, that Pickett became known as one of the great soul singers of the Sixties with hits such as 'Mustang Sally', '634-5789' and 'In The Midnight Hour'. It was at the suggestion of guitarist Duane Allman that Pickett recorded 'Hey Jude' in 1969 and managed to have a hit with it at the same time that the Beatles' version was in the charts.

On the recording of 'You Can't Do That', John played lead on his newly-acquired Rickenbacker while George played 12-string guitar for the first time on a Beatles' record. "I find it a drag to play rhythm guitar all the time," John told *Melody Maker*. "I like to work out something interesting to play. The best example is what I did on 'You Can't Do That'. There wasn't really a lead guitarist and a rhythm guitarist on that because...rhythm guitar is too thin for records."

Recorded at Abbey Road after returning from their first visit to America it was used in the TV show sequence of *A Hard Day's Night* but didn't make the final cut.

Perennial magpies, the Beatles were inspired by musicians as diverse as Wilson Pickett and Del Shannon.

**YOU CAN'T
DO THAT
Written:**
Lennon/
McCartney
Length: 2' 37"
UK single release:
March 20, 1964 as
B-side of 'Can't
Buy Me Love'
US single release:
March 16, 1964 as
B-side of 'Can't
Buy Me Love'

I'LL BE BACK

John found the chords for 'I'll Be Back' while playing a Del Shannon song. This was probably 'Runaway', which the Beatles had played in their early shows and which also starts with a minor chord and has a descending bass line.

Shannon had hits in 1961 and 1962 with 'Runaway', 'Hats Off To Larry', 'So Long Baby' and 'Hey Little Girl'. In 1963, after a hit with 'Little Town Flirt', he played London's Royal Albert Hall (April 18) with the Beatles and suggested to them that he could help expose their work in America by covering one of their songs as a single.

The Beatles agreed and Shannon went back home and recorded a version of 'From Me To You' which, although it only reached Number 77, was the first Lennon and McCartney composition to feature in the American charts.

The song was originally recorded in 3/4 waltz time but John found it too difficult to sing so he altered it to 4/4 time.

I'LL BE BACK

Written:	Lennon/McCartney
Length:	2' 20"
UK release:	*A Hard Day's Night* album, July 10, 1964
US release:	*Beatles '65* album, December 15, 1964

BEATLES FOR SALE

The *Beatles For Sale* sleeve revealed the flip side of Beatlemania – the exhaustion, bewilderment and loneliness of life at the top. John, Paul, George and Ringo look frazzled and world-weary in Robert Freeman's cover photographs and, the same pressurized feeling coloured their new songs. They only had time to write eight of the album's 14 tracks. Covers of their early rock'n'roll favourites were used to fill out the quota.

The songs they did write showed all the signs of having been written in the hothouse of fame. Although 'Eight Days a Week' was a love song, its title was inspired by a comment on overwork. John's songs were bleaker than anything he'd written before, with 'I'm A Loser' offering a foretaste of his confessional style of songwriting. For 'I'll Follow The Sun', Paul had to go back through his old school notebooks to polish up a song he'd last played in the Cavern days.

Bob Dylan, who Paul and John both heard and met for the first time during 1964, was beginning to be an influence. In the early days, the Beatles had concentrated mainly on mastering the musical side of the songs – chord changes, arrangements, harmonies and delivery. Dylan was the first recording artist to affect them primarily as lyricists. Initially, Paul was the big Dylan fan, but John soon caught up with him.

John had been writing poems and short stories for years, mostly for the amusement of friends. Some of these were published in his book *In His Own Write* in 1964, when he was hailed by the press as 'the literary Beatle' and comparisons of his work were made with that of Lewis Carroll, Edward Lear and the James Joyce of *Finnegan's Wake*. Dylan, and later the British journalist Kenneth Allsop, impressed

The rushed *Beatles For Sale* album saw the band stressed by the pressures of their fame and feral Beatlemania.

upon him the need to close the gap between his 'literary' outpourings and lyric writing. John interpreted this to mean that, "Instead of projecting myself into a situation, I would try to express what I felt about myself (as I had done) in my book."

The group's press officer Derek Taylor was surely right when he wrote in the sleeve notes; "The kids of AD 2000 will draw from the music much the same sense of wellbeing and warmth as we do today. For the magic of the Beatles is, I suspect, timeless and ageless… it is adored by the world."

Beatles For Sale took two and a half months to record and was released in December 1964, reaching Number 1 in Britain. The American equivalent, *Beatles '65*, also hit the top spot and sold a million copies in the first week.

I FEEL FINE

The Beatles completed the album *A Hard Day's Night* in June 1964 and by mid-August were back in the studio to start work on *Beatles For Sale*. On August 19, they left Britain to tour America and returned a month later to work on *Beatles For Sale*. *A Hard Day's Night* had been the first album to consist solely of Lennon and McCartney songs but, with so little time between projects, they found it impossible to come up with enough original material for *Beatles For Sale*.

On October 6, while recording 'Eight Days A Week', John was working out the guitar riff that would become the basis of 'I Feel Fine', a song they recorded only 12 days later. It was obviously inspired by Bobby Parker's riff on his 1961 track 'Watch Your Step'. "I actually wrote 'I Feel Fine' around the riff which is going on in the background," John said in December 1964. "I tried to get that effect into every song on the LP, but the others wouldn't have it.

"I told them that I'd write a song specially for this riff so they said, 'Yes. You go away and do that,' knowing that we'd almost finished the album. Anyway, going into the studio one morning I said to Ringo, 'I've written this song but it's lousy', but we tried it, complete with riff, and it sounded like an A side, so we decided to release it just like that."

Apart from the riff, the distinctive feature of 'I Feel Fine' is the sound of feedback from John's guitar that blends into the opening chords. It was one of those discoveries that they made in the studio and decided to use on a track because they liked it. John's semi-acoustic Gibson guitar was leaning against an amplifier after a take of a song and an electronic whine was set up. This along with other innovations on *Beatles For Sale* was a significant development in their approach to recording. Having mastered the studio basics, they were now encouraging George

I FEEL FINE

Written:	Lennon/McCartney
Length:	2' 20"
UK single release:	November 27, 1964
UK chart position:	1
US single release:	November 23, 1964
US chart position:	1

Martin to take risks and were finding fresh sources of inspiration in noises that would previously have been eliminated as mistakes (electronic goofs, twisted tapes, talkback). Feedback was to become a familiar part of recording – used by artists such as Jimi Hendrix and the Who – and John remained proud of the fact that the Beatles were the first group to purposefully put it on a record.

'I Feel Fine', John's most optimistic song to date, became a Number 1 single in both Britain and America.

As the Beatles topped charts in Britain and the US, transatlantic flights became part of a wearying routine.

SHE'S A WOMAN

'She's A Woman' was conceived by Paul on the streets of St John's Wood on October 8, 1964 and was finished the same day in the studio, Paul performing it in the high-pitched scream which he adopted to emulate Little Richard. It was a conscious decision to bring a more bluesy sound to the Beatles. Some lines and the middle eight were added by John. "We needed a real screaming rocker for the live act," said Paul. "It was always good if you were stuck for something to close with or if there was a dull moment."

On the early takes Paul improvised extensively. Take 7, for example, lasted almost six and a half minutes, and contained lots of ad libs and screams. At the end Paul can be heard saying, "We've got a song and an instrumental there!" Unfortunately the song also contained one of the most strained rhymes in the Beatles songbook when 'present' was matched with 'she's no peasant'.

'She's A Woman' was also the first Beatles' song to contain a veiled drug reference. John later confessed that they were quite proud to have inserted the line 'turns me on when I get lonely' and for it to have escaped the attention of the broadcast censors. When they used the phrase 'turn you on' three years later (in 'A Day In The Life'), it led to a radio ban: by then, the authorities had become aware of the growing drug culture and its terminology.

Significantly, it was just five weeks before recording 'She's A Woman' that the Beatles had smoked marijuana for the first time. Until then, their only experience of drugs had been Drinamyl and Preludin tablets that they'd discovered in Hamburg and the strips from Benzedrine inhalers that they'd been shown in Liverpool. They were introduced to marijuana in the company of Bob Dylan, who met them for the first time in their suite at the Delmonico

SHE'S A WOMAN
Written: Lennon/ McCartney
Length: 2' 57"
UK single release: November 27, 1964 as B-side of 'I Feel Fine'
US single release: November 23, 1964 as B-side of 'I Feel Fine'

'She's A Woman' saw the Beatles make their first hidden reference to drugs in a song after they were initated in the joys of marijuana by Bob Dylan.

Hotel in New York City. The Beatles were happy to drink cheap wine into the small hours, but Dylan wanted to smoke a joint and assumed that they were all dope smokers because he mistakenly thought they had sung 'I get high', instead of 'I can't hide' in 'I Want To Hold Your Hand'.

The Beatles were apprehensive about joining in at first, but before long the lights were lowered, candles and incense were lit and towels were stuffed along the bottoms of the doors. For the next few hours, the musicians were "legless with laughing" as George Harrison later put it. Paul thought that he'd suddenly been blessed with amazing insights and even went to the trouble of recording his insights on a notepad.

'She's A Woman' was released as the B side of 'I Feel Fine' in Britain and America. "At first, it wasn't so well received," said Paul in 1965. "A lot of people thought that I was just singing too high and that I'd picked the wrong key. It sounded as though I was screeching, but it was on purpose. It wasn't a mistake."

EIGHT DAYS A WEEK

John always claimed that 'Eight Days A Week' was written by Paul as a potential title track for the Beatles' follow-up film to *A Hard Day's Night*.

Director Dick Lester denied this, pointing out that 'Eight Days A Week' was recorded in October 1964, whereas filming on *Help!* didn't begin until late February 1965. It's unlikely that they were considering film music this far in advance. "The film was always supposed to be called *Help* but there was a copyright problem in that someone else had registered this title," says Lester. "So we originally called it *Beatles II* and then *Eight Arms To Hold You,* but the possibility of having to write a song called 'Eight Arms to Hold You' had everyone throwing their hands in the air and saying that it was impossible. It was because of this that we thought, sod it, we'll take the chance, because the laws of registration were so vague. We decided to stick in an exclamation mark because the one that was registered didn't have one."

EIGHT DAYS A WEEK
Written: Lennon/McCartney
Length: 2' 45"
UK release: *Beatles For Sale* album, December 4, 1964
US single release: February 15, 1965
US chart position: 1

Paul heard the phrase 'eight days a week' from a chauffeur who drove him to John's home in Weybridge one day for a writing session. Asked by Paul if he had been busy lately the chauffeur replied, "Busy? I've been working eight days a week." When they arrived in Weybridge Paul went straight in and told John that he had the title for the song they were going to write that day. American radio DJ Larry Kane, who accompanied the Beatles on their 1964 US tour, claims in his book that he heard the group running through the tune on a flight between Dallas and New York on September 20.

'Eight Days A Week', the first track to be recorded with a fade-in, was under consideration as a single in Britain until John came up with 'I Feel Fine'. In America, it was released as the follow-up to 'I Feel Fine' and made the Number 1 spot.

The Beatles managed to maintain standards of prodigious creativity despite being at the heart of relentless media attention and their fans' adulation.

I'M A LOSER

Two events during 1964 were to have a profound effect on John's writing. The first was hearing Bob Dylan's music in Paris during January, when Paul acquired *The Freewheelin' Bob Dylan* from an interviewer at a local radio station.

Paul had heard Dylan's music before through his student friends in Liverpool but it was the first time John had heard it. After hearing *Freewheelin'*, which was Dylan's second album, they went out and bought his debut album *Bob Dylan* and, according to John, "for the rest of our three weeks we didn't stop playing them. We all went potty on Dylan."

The second event to affect John in a big way was meeting the journalist Kenneth Allsop, a writer for the *Daily Mail* and a regular interviewer on BBC Television's news magazine programme *Tonight*. John first met him on March 23, and then again at a Foyles Literary Luncheon at the Dorchester Hotel in London's Park Lane and later that day was interviewed for four minutes on *Tonight* about his book *In His Own Write*. Allsop, a handsome craggy Yorkshireman, was 44 years old at the time and about to become one of the best-known faces on British television. He had been in journalism since 1938, with a brief interruption caused by the war, during which he served in the Royal Air Force.

It was in the 'green room', the hospitality suite, at the BBC's Lime Grove Studios on March 23 that Allsop first spoke to John about his songwriting, encouraging him not to hide his true feelings behind the conventions of the pop song. It was obvious to Allsop from reading *In His Own Write* that John had much more to give if he was prepared to explore his deeper feelings.

Years later, John told his confidant Elliot Mintz that this meeting marked a significant turning point in his songwriting. "He told me

After John and Paul were exposed to the music of Bob Dylan in 1964, they 'went potty on Dylan' for weeks.

that he was very nervous that day and, because of this, became very talkative and engaged Allsop in conversation," says Mintz.

"Allsop had in essence said to him that he wasn't terribly enamoured with Beatles' songs because they all tended to be 'she loves him', 'he loves her', 'they love her' and 'I love her'. He suggested to John that he try to write something more autobiographical, based on personal experience rather than these abstract images. That struck a chord with him."

Although recorded five months later, 'I'm A Loser' was the first fruit of this meeting with Allsop. It would be wrong to say it was a complete change of direction, because from the beginning John had written songs in which he exposed himself as lonely, sad and abandoned, but in 'I'm A Loser' he let a little more of his true self show. On the surface, it's another song about having lost a girl but the lines that announce that beneath his mask he is 'wearing a frown', suggest that he considers himself a loser in more ways than one. He's not just a loser in love; he feels that he's a loser in life.

All this would be idle speculation if not for the fact that 'I'm A Loser' can now be seen as an early stage in John's tortuous journey towards candid self-revelation in his songwriting. At the time, he was quick to credit the effect Bob Dylan had on 'I'm A Loser'. "Anyone who is one of the best in his field – as Dylan is – is bound to

The incessant demands of superstardom took their toll on the band's equanimity: 'Sometimes I wonder how the hell we keep it up,' admitted John.

influence people," he said at the time. "I wouldn't be surprised if we influenced him in some way."

Kenneth Allsop went on to present the television news programme *24 Hours* and then, in May 1973, he was found dead at his home. The cause of his death was an overdose of painkillers but the lack of a suicide note meant that the inquest recorded an open verdict.

Hard Travellin', Allsop's account of the life of the American hobo which was first published in 1967, has become a classic of its kind and is still in print.

'I'm a Loser' was recorded in August 1964. The honesty of the song's confession can be proved by a comment John made to Ray Coleman of *Melody Maker* two months later while backstage before a concert. "I wish I could paint a smile on too," he said as he applied stage make-up. "Don't you think I'll manage one tonight? Sometimes, I wonder how the hell we keep it up."

I'M A LOSER
Written: Lennon/McCartney
Length: 2' 33"
UK release: *Beatles For Sale* album, December 4, 1964
US release: *Beatles '65* album, December 15, 1964

NO REPLY

'No Reply' was a typical John song of betrayal and jealousy; a story of a girl taking off with another guy. It was based, he once said, not on his own experience but on 'Silhouettes', a big hit in 1957 for the Rays on Philadelphia's independent Cameo label. Written by Bob Crewe and Frank Slaye, who went on to write hits for Freddy Cannon, 'Silhouettes' put a new twist on the old love cheat story: the boy discovers he is being two-timed when he notices the silhouettes on the curtains of his lover's house.

In John's version, the boy becomes suspicious when his girl doesn't answer the door and, when he calls her on the phone, her parents tell him she's not at home. As in 'Silhouettes', he returns to her house and, watching from the shadows, sees her go in 'with another man'. His repetition of the line 'I saw the light', referring to the light behind the curtain but also to the revelation that he was being two-timed, could possibly be an allusion to Hank Williams' well-known song of personal salvation 'I Saw The Light' (1948).

Ever since 'Please Please Me', the Beatles' compositions had been published by Northern Songs, a company set up by John, Paul, Brian Epstein and music publisher Dick James, who was a friend of George Martin. James had experience both as singer and songwriter before getting into publishing and, when he heard 'No Reply', he said to John: "That's the first complete song you've written, the first song which resolves itself. It's a complete story."

NO REPLY
Written:
Lennon/
McCartney
Length: 2' 17"
UK release:
Beatles For Sale
album, December
4, 1964
US release:
Beatles '65 album,
December 15,
1964

97

I DON'T WANT TO SPOIL THE PARTY

The Beatles briefly visited America in February 1964, playing in Washington DC and New York City to promote 'I Want To Hold Your Hand' and doing live TV shows for Ed Sullivan in New York and Miami. It wasn't until August 1964 that they arrived for their first full-fledged tour, a month-long trek that would take them to 20 US cities plus three in Canada. Playing 12 songs per show, they were supported by four American acts – the Bill Black Combo, the Exciters, Jackie DeShannon and the Righteous Brothers.

It is highly likely that John wrote 'I Don't Want To Spoil The Party' in Los Angeles the night of August 24th 1964. Of the eight self-written songs on the album two had already been written before the tour ('Baby's In Black' and 'I'm A Loser') and two were written in Britain on their return ('Eight Days A Week' and 'She's A Woman'). That leaves four songs that must have been written on the tour. Paul told an interviewer that he had written two songs when staying at the La Fayette Motor Inn in Atlantic City. That leaves two songs for which John would have been the primary writer and the best guess is 'No Reply' and 'I Don't Want To Spoil The Party'.

I DON'T WANT TO SPOIL THE PARTY

Written: Lennon/McCartney
Length: 2' 36"
US single release: February 15, 1965, as B-side of 'Eight Days A Week'

The Beatles played the *Ed Sullivan Show* on US TV in February 1964 before playing a full tour later that year.

The evidence for 'I Don't Want To Spoil The Party' being written in LA is that we know from contemporary accounts that John stayed in on the night of the 24th to write a song. We also know that in order to do so he turned down an invitation to a party at Burt Lancaster's house that George, Paul and Ringo went to. It would make sense that John's mind would turn to the subject of being a party pooper.

The two days in LA had been particularly stressful for the Beatles. They had arrived the day before at 03:55, flown in from Vancouver, and had been housed in a mansion at 356 St Pierre Road owned by British actor Reginald Owens. They gave a press conference for over 200 journalists the first day and then in the evening played at the Hollywood Bowl. Later there had been a party at the mansion where John had been locked in conversation with Joan Baez.

The next day the Beatles had to pump flesh for an hour at a charity garden party for the Haemophilia Foundation. Adults could only attend if they brought a child. It was just the sort of event that John hated because he had to play the role of the cheerful Beatle.

This might have put him in just the mood to write a song about his inability to pretend that he's enjoying himself. Significantly when discussing the song later he said it was "deeply personal" to him.

I'LL FOLLOW THE SUN

The contrast between John and Paul's outlook on life and love could hardly have been greater. Whereas John usually saw himself as a victim, Paul felt himself to be in charge of life. In 'If I Fell', John demanded a promise that love would last. In 'I'll Follow The Sun', Paul accepts that no such guarantee is possible. He knows that stormy weather may hit his relationship and so he makes plans to follow the sun. A selfish song in a way because it doesn't consider how the abandoned girl might find her own sunshine, it was nonetheless an accurate reflection of Paul's romantic life.

Polished up for use when the pressure was on for the Beatles to come up with their own material, the song was originally written in 1959 at Forthlin Road. There was a wave of interest in Buddy Holly following his death that gave him four hit singles in Britain before the year was out. In 'I'll Follow The Sun', it's easy to detect the effect that he had on the young Paul McCartney. Holly was a significant influence on the Beatles because, unlike Elvis, he wrote all his own songs and had a permanent, identifiable backing group. John (who was short-sighted) was encouraged

I'LL FOLLOW THE SUN

Written: Lennon/McCartney
Length: 1' 51"
UK release: *Beatles For Sale* album, December 4, 1964
US release: *Beatles '65* album, December 15, 1964

Paul shows Ed Sullivan a few basic chords before the Beatles play his TV show, 1964.

that a bespectacled singer could become a rock'n'roll star and the initial naming of the group 'Beetles' was inspired by Buddy's Crickets.

Beatles For Sale included a Chuck Berry track ('Rock And Roll Music'), a Leiber and Stoller ('Kansas City'), a Little Richard ('Hey, Hey, Hey'), a Buddy Holly ('Words Of Love') and two songs by Carl Perkins ('Honey Don't' and 'Everybody's Trying To Be My Baby'), all of them recorded hurriedly towards the end of the sessions. "There are still one or two of our very early numbers which are worth recording," Paul explained to *Mersey Beat* at the time. "Every now and then we remember one of the good ones we wrote in the early days and one of them, 'I'll Follow The Sun', is on the LP."

In the Seventies, Paul's company MPL Communications bought Holly's publishing catalogue and has since been responsible for organizing an annual Buddy Holly Day.

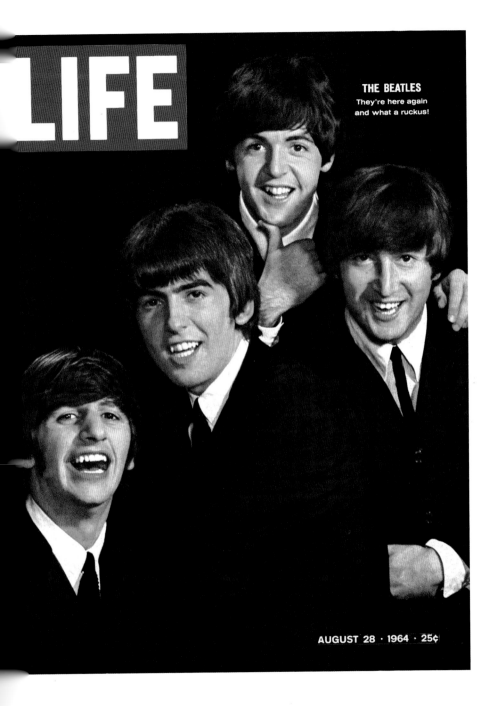

LIFE

THE BEATLES
They're here again
and what a ruckus!

AUGUST 28 · 1964 · 25¢

BABY'S IN BLACK

"They're here again and what a ruckus!" proclaimed *Time* as the Beatles began their US tour in August 1964.

**BABY'S IN
BLACK
Written:**
Lennon/
McCartney
Length: 2' 07"
UK release:
Beatles For Sale
album, December
4, 1964
US release:
Beatles '65 album,
December 15,
1964

A simple song with a simple story. Boy loves girl, girl loves other boy, other boy doesn't love girl. Girl is sad and therefore dresses in black.

By 1964, Lennon and McCartney seldom sat together and wrote a song from start to finish as they had done so often in the past. Even though some songs were still collaborations, this now usually meant that an unfinished song was given a middle eight by the other partner or awkward lines were improved. The nose-to-nose writing that had happened in Liverpool and during the early days in London was coming to an end. "It would be daft to sit around waiting for a partner to finish your song off with you," explained Paul at the time. "If you happen to be on your own, you might as well get it finished yourself. If I get stuck on the middle eight of a new number, I give up, knowing that when I see John he will finish it off for me. He'll bring a new approach to it and that particular song will finish up half and half, Lennon and McCartney."

'Baby's In Black' was a genuine joint effort, the first since 'I Want To Hold Your Hand' almost a year before, with John and Paul writing the song together in the same room at Kenwood. According to Paul it was another attempt to write something "a little bit darker, bluesy…" It became the first song to be recorded for *Beatles For Sale*.

EVERY LITTLE THING

'Every Little Thing', was written by Paul for Jane Asher and had much the same theme as 'Things We Said Today'. Reflecting the values of the era it tells the tale of a lucky guy whose girl loves him so much she does everything for him.

Paul wrote 'Every Little Thing' for his girlfriend, Jane Asher, while living at the Asher family home in London.

It's another song which wouldn't go down so well in the Nineties because the girl's needs are not even considered, the assumption being that she should find her fulfilment in serving her man. Ironically, it was the attitudes expressed in this song that Jane Asher later challenged when she told Paul she need to find fulfilment in her acting career. It wasn't enough for her to be simply the girlfriend of one of the world's most desirable pop stars; she wanted to make her own mark in the world of the arts.

Although this song was credited solely to Paul who had come up with the basis for the track in his room at the Asher family home in Wimpole Street, John remembered that he might have "thrown something in" too. It was an attempt at writing a single, but became an album track.

EVERY LITTLE THING

Written:	Lennon/McCartney
Length:	2' 04''
UK release:	*Beatles For Sale* album, December 4, 1964
US release:	*Beatles '65* album, December 15, 1964

WHAT YOU'RE DOING

Although 'What You're Doing' tells a fairly straightforward story of a boy being given the runaround by his girl, the lyric contains some inventive rhyming in 'doing' and 'blue an', 'running' and 'fun in'. The most memorable part of the arrangement was the Beatles shouting the first word of each verse, with Paul completing the phrases. It was possibly one of two songs that Paul started while staying at the La Fayette Motor Inn in Atlantic City on August 31st 1964.

Tim Riley, author of a book about the Beatles' music entitled *Tell Me Why*, praised the track for its pop ingenuity, saying that the addition of piano for just the guitar solo and the final fade-out suggested a love of detail that they were later to develop more fully: "The Beatles' conception of what the studio allowed them to do in altering textures and changing musical colours is emerging as a stylistic trait, not just a gimmick."

'What You're Doing' was another song written by Paul specifically for *Beatles For Sale* with additions from John. The recording was quite painstaking, beginning in September 1964 and picking up again in late October, at which time the track was completely re-made. Paul's final verdict was that it was a better recording than it was a song.

WHAT YOU'RE DOING

Written:
Lennon/
McCartney
Length: 2' 34"
UK release:
Beatles For Sale
album, December
4, 1964
US release:
Beatles VI album,
June 14, 1965

HELP!

The Beatles' second feature film was shot between February and May 1965 at a number of locations including New Providence Island in the Bahamas, the Austrian Alps, London's Cliveden House and Twickenham Film Studios.

The original script was by American Marc Behm who wanted Ringo to play a man who mistakenly signs his own death warrant and is pursued by a homicidal maniac played by Peter Sellers.

"We were just about to begin shooting when I learned that Philip de Brocca was filming the very same story – *The Troubles of a Chinaman in China* starring Jean-Paul Belmondo," says Behm. "I rushed to my pads and pencils and in a day or so wrote another script, *The Indian Giver*. It was this script that Richard Lester asked Charles Wood to do an 'English draft' of because he considered mine too American!"

Ringo was still the main protagonist in the rewrite where he was cast as the inheritor of a magic ring pursued by members of an evil cult. Again, all the songs, apart from the title track, were written with no knowledge of the script and dropped into the film at appropriate points. Dick Lester was given a tape of the songs and chose the six that he considered would best fit.

The Beatles later expressed dissatisfaction with *Help!*, saying that they'd been no more than extras in their own film. However, it was to mark the beginning of undoubtedly their most fertile period of songwriting.

John wrote the film's title track, using the word 'help' to explore his insecurity: it was to remain one of his favourite Beatles' songs. Paul's 'Yesterday', which was used on the non-soundtrack side of the

The Beatles were to express dissatisfaction with 1965 movie *Help!*, saying they had been 'no more than extras in their own film'.

album, went on to become the most covered of all the Beatles' songs and the first to be regarded as a classic.

Having discovered pot during the previous year, the Beatles were now smoking the drug regularly and John remembered this as their 'pot period', describing how reels of film had to be scrapped because all they featured were the Beatles in fits of uncontrollable laughter.

Help!, the album, was released in August 1965 and topped the charts in Britain and America. As with *A Hard Day's Night*, the American version consisted only of the songs in the film plus a few tracks by George Martin and an orchestra.

YES IT IS

Posing with a piano (and a mysterious 'third leg' behind George) while shooting *Help!* in the Swiss Alps in 1965.

John spoke about having once written love songs purely for 'the meat market' and yet it's hard to find the songs he was referring to. 'Yes It Is', though, was one song he felt particularly embarrassed about in later years, scoffing at the line 'for red is the colour that will make me blue'. John claimed that it was nothing more than an attempt to rewrite 'This Boy' as it had the same chords, harmonies and "double-Dutch words".

The lyric is a warning to a girl not to wear red because this is the colour that the singer's 'baby' always wore. John's final verdict on the song was that "it didn't work".

It was released as the B side to 'Ticket To Ride' in both Britain and America during April 1965.

YES IT IS

Written: Lennon/McCartney
Length: 2' 42"
UK single release: April 9, 1965 as B-side of 'Ticket To Ride'
US chart release: April 19, 1965 as B-side of 'Ticket To Ride'

I'M DOWN

The B side of the single 'Help!', 'I'm Down' is an unashamed attempt by Paul to write a Little Richard song with which to replace 'Long Tall Sally' in the Beatles' set. "We spent a lot of time trying to write a real corker – something like 'Long Tall Sally'", Paul said in October 1964. "It's very difficult. 'I Saw Her Standing There' was the nearest we got to it. We're still trying to compose a Little Richard sort of song. I'd liken it to abstract painting. People think of 'Long Tall Sally' and say it sounds so easy to write. But it's the most difficult thing we've attempted. Writing a three-chord song that's clever is not easy."

'She's A Woman', although not as frenetic, was a similar attempt to get into the Little Richard mode but Paul always felt culturally disadvantaged because he hadn't been exposed to gospel music during his formative years. Church of England choirs and Salvation Army bands didn't quite provide the same sort of education for writing barn-storming rock'n'roll.

Little Richard, who'd had his first British hit with 'Rip It Up' in 1956, met the Beatles when they shared a bill at the Tower Ballroom,

I'M DOWN

Written:	Lennon/McCartney
Length:	2' 31"
UK single release:	July 23, 1965 as B-side of 'I'm Down'
US single release:	July 19, 1965 as B-side of 'I'm Down'

New Brighton, on October 12, 1962, one week after the release of 'Love Me Do'. It was a great moment for the group, who had featured 'Rip It Up', 'Good Golly Miss Molly', 'Tutti Frutti', 'Lucille' among several Little Richard numbers in their shows.

"I met them in Liverpool before the world ever knew about them," says Little Richard. "Paul especially was into my music and had been playing it since he was in high school. He was impressed with my hollerin' and, when I was on stage in Liverpool and later in Hamburg (at the Star Club the following month), he used to stay in the wings and watch me sing. I felt honoured that they liked my music. My style is very dynamic. It's full of joy, it's full of fun and it's alive. There is nothing dead about it. There's never a dull moment. It keeps you on your toes, it keeps you movin' and I think that's what everybody gets from my music. People know that if they sing one of my songs on stage, they're gonna light up the house."

Fittingly, the Beatles used 'I'm Down' to close the show during their 1965 and 1966 tours. The last song they ever played live in concert, though, at San Francisco's Candlestick Park on August 29, 1966, was Little Richard's 'Long Tall Sally'.

The band tread water in the swimming pool at the Nassau Beach Hotel while filming *Help!* in the Bahamas.

HELP!

As soon as he had embarked on his solo career in the Seventies, John would often refer to 'Help!' as one of his favourite Beatles' songs. He liked it, he said, because it was "real". His sole regret was that, for commercial reasons, they had changed it from a slow Dylanesque number into a jolly Beatles' tune.

'Help!' was written with Paul at John's Weybridge home, Kenwood, in April 1965. The lyric was a candid insight into John's dissatisfaction with himself. He was eating and drinking too much, had put on weight and felt trapped by fame. The song, he would later admit, really was a cry for help, despite being written to order for the film. "I needed the help," he said. "The song was about me."

Putting his feelings at the centre of a song, wasn't so much a departure as it was a consolidation of the self-examination that had always lurked beneath even the most innocent-sounding of his songs. The only difference was that now he seemed to be admitting that fame, wealth and success had heightened rather than relieved his anxiety.

At the pinnacle of pop stardom, John had started to look back with longing to what he now saw as those relatively uncomplicated days at Menlove Avenue. The idealization of his boyhood and adolescence was a theme that was to grow in significance in his songwriting.

Maureen Cleave, the London journalist who had helped out on the lyrics for A Hard Day's Night, felt that John should start to use words of more than one syllable. 'Help!' was his first serious attempt to do this, and he managed to incorporate 'self-assured', 'appreciate', 'independence' and 'insecure' within the song. (Maureen Cleave was actually at Weybridge, visiting Cynthia, when the song was being written.)

In the film *Help!*, again directed by Dick Lester, the song was used in the title sequence, where black and white footage of the Beatles was projected on to a screen set up in the temple of the religious cult.

Despite being the main protagonist of *Help!*, Ringo looks less than enamoured of his lot as filming continues on Salisbury Plain.

HELP!

Written: Lennon/McCartney
Length: 2' 21"
UK single release: July 23, 1965
UK chart position: 1
US single release: July 19, 1965
US chart position: 1

THE NIGHT BEFORE

As with *A Hard Day's Night*, the songs used in *Help!* owed nothing to the script. "I think all the songs in *Help!* were written before the screenplay was even completed," confirms Dick Lester. "I was given a demo tape with about eleven songs and I chose six of them in a rather arbitrary way, thinking that they were ones which I could do something with. It was as casual as that and I fitted the songs into the film in places where I thought I could do something with them."

Composed as a song of regret over a love lost, Paul was filmed singing 'The Night Before' while surrounded by troops and tanks on Salisbury Plain. The track was recorded in February 1965 and filmed three months later.

113

THE NIGHT BEFORE

Written:	Lennon/McCartney
Length:	2' 36''
UK release:	*Help!* album, August 6, 1965
US release:	*Help!* album, August 13, 1965

YOU'VE GOT TO HIDE YOUR LOVE AWAY

Bob Dylan's music – (the acoustic *Another Side Of Bob Dylan* was his most recent album) – directed John towards a more intense and personal style of writing. He began to write songs in which his state of mind became the immediate starting point. In the first lines of 'You've Got To Hide Your Love Away', the image of John standing facing a wall with his head in his hands was probably a perfect description of how he felt when he was writing.

The song is about a relationship that has gone wrong and John's hidden feelings for a girl he has lost. Tony Bramwell suggests that it was written for Brian Epstein, warning him to keep his homosexual relationships (which, at the time, were illegal in Britain) from public view. It was also rumoured that it referred to a secret affair John was having.

Written by John at Kenwood, it was used in the film during a scene in which British actress Eleanor Bron visited the group in their terraced house to retrieve the missing ring.

John's childhood friend, Pete Shotton, was with him at Kenwood and remembered that in the original version he had sung that he felt 'two foot tall'. However, when he sang it to Paul, he mistakenly sang 'two foot small', which Paul liked better and so it was kept. Shotton went to the recording on February 18, 1965, and added some 'heys' to the chorus.

YOU'VE GOT TO HIDE YOUR LOVE AWAY
Written:
Lennon/
McCartney
Length: 2' 11"
UK release:
Help! album,
August 6, 1965
US release:
Help! album,
August 13, 1965

I NEED YOU

I NEED YOU
Written:
Harrison
Length: 2' 31"
UK release:
Help! album,
August 6, 1965
US release:
Help! album,
August 13, 1965

A formulaic love song, 'I Need You' was written by George for his girlfriend Pattie Boyd, and was one of two of his Beatles' songs which he didn't comment on in his 1980 book *I Me Mine* (the other was 'You Like Me Too Much').

It was also the only George song to be featured in the film *Help!* (in the Salisbury Plain sequence) and the first to use a wah-wah pedal to distort the guitar sound.

Some Beatles' books have claimed that George wrote it in the Bahamas while separated from Pattie, but this can't be true as recording began on February 15, 1965, and these Bahamian scenes weren't shot until the following week.

George wrote 'I Need You' for Pattie Boyd but it is one of the less distinguished numbers in the Beatles' canon.

ANOTHER GIRL

'Another Girl' was written by Paul during a ten-day holiday in Tunisia and used in a scene filmed on Balmoral Island in the Bahamas.

In this song, Paul talks about being under pressure to commit long-term to his girlfriend but how he's not going to do this, mainly because he's already got himself another girl. This may have been a reference to the fact that although he was still firmly linked to Jane Asher in the public mind he was also seeing other women.

Speaking to Barry Miles for his authorised biography *Many Years From Now* Paul wrongly identified the villa as British Embassy property. It was actually Sebastian's Villa built in the coastal resort of Hammanet in the 1920s by George Sebastian. The Moorish-style building was later described by the great American architect Frank Lloyd Wright as "the most beautiful house I know." It was visited by Ernest Hemingway, F. Scott Fitzgerald and King Edward VII. During the war is was requisitioned by Rommell and then Churchill stayed there. It was gifted to the Tunisian state in 1959 and in 1964 an amphitheatre was added in the grounds. It was in the villa's huge sunken bath surrounded by colonnades that Paul wrote the song. Sebastian's Villa is now Hammanet's International Cultural Centre.

John once said that the Beatles' songs were like signatures; even when they weren't trying to give anything away they would betray their most fund-amental attitudes. "It was always apparent – if you looked below the surface – what was being said. Resentfulness or love or hate, it's apparent in all our work."

'Another Girl' was recorded the day after Paul returned from his holiday.

ANOTHER GIRL
Written:
Lennon/
McCartney
Length: 2' 08"
UK release:
Help! album,
August 6, 1965
US release:
Help! album,
August 13, 1965

YOU'RE GOING TO LOSE THAT GIRL

YOU'RE GOING TO LOSE THAT GIRL
Written:
Lennon/
McCartney
Length: 2' 20"
UK release:
Help! album,
August 6, 1965
US release:
Help! album,
August 13, 1965

The Beatles sang 'You're Going To Lose That Girl' in a scene in *Help!* set in the recording studio, which was actually filmed at Twickenham Film Studios. The song is interrupted when the gang chasing Ringo cut a hole around his drum kit from the ceiling of the room below.

Written mainly by John but completed with Paul at Weybridge, it is a warning to an unidentified male that if he doesn't start treating his girlfriend right, he (John) is going to move in on her, developing a theme he first outlined in 'She Loves You'.

Despite its comedic use in *Help!*, 'That Girl' developed a menacing lyrical theme John had first explored in 'She Loves You'.

TICKET TO RIDE

Ringo, complete with the tools of his trade, peers from a carriage window during the filming of the promo for 'Ticket To Ride'.

'Ticket To Ride' was written by John and Paul as a single and was described by John as "one of the earliest heavy metal records made". Although they were pipped at the post in the heavy metal stakes by the Kinks' 'You Really Got Me', this was the first Beatles' track to feature an insistent, clanking riff underpinned by a heavy drum beat and it used a fade-out with an altered melody.

Used in *Help!*, during the Austrian snow scenes, it was released as a single in April 1965 and had already topped the charts in Britain and America by the time the film came out. Paul confessed to his biographer Barry Miles that the apparently loopy suggestion made by some American Beatles' fans at the time that the song was referring to a British Railways ticket to the town of Ryde on the Isle of Wight was partly right. Paul's cousin Betty Robbins and her husband Mike ran the Bow Bars in Union Street, Ryde, and Paul and John had visited them there. Although the song was primarily about a girl riding out of the life of the narrator, they were conscious of the potential for a double meaning.

Don Short, a show business journalist who travelled extensively with the Beatles in the Sixties, was told by John that the phrase had yet another meaning. "The girls who worked the streets in Hamburg had to have a clean bill of health and so the medical authorities would give them a card saying that they didn't have a dose of anything," says Short. "I was with the Beatles when they went back to Hamburg in June 1966 and it was then that John told me that he had coined the phrase 'a ticket to ride' to describe these cards. He could have been joking – you always had to be careful with John like that – but I certainly remember him telling me that."

TICKET TO RIDE
Written:
Lennon/
McCartney
Length: 3' 12"
UK single release:
April 9, 1965
UK chart
position: 1
US chart release:
April 19, 1965
US chart
position: 1

TELL ME WHAT YOU SEE

'Tell Me What You See' was another 'work song' by Paul who asks his girl to give her heart to him because he's utterly trustworthy and will brighten up her life. If she doesn't believe him, he suggests that she take a look in his eyes and tell him what she sees.

The track was recorded before the filming of *Help!* and offered to Dick Lester for the soundtrack, but was rejected. Obviously, he was not too keen on what he heard. Tim Riley, in his book about the Beatles' music, notes that it is one of the album's weaker songs, suggesting that it became a working draft for the altogether stronger track 'I'm Looking Through You'.

TELL ME WHAT YOU SEE

Written: Lennon/McCartney
Length: 2' 39"
UK release: *Help!* album, August 6, 1965
US release: *Beatles VI* album, June 14, 1965

YOU LIKE
ME TOO MUCH

'You Like Me Too Much' was written and recorded by George for the soundtrack and recorded before filming started on *Help!* It was eventually relegated to the B side of the album.

George chose not to discuss 'You Like Me Too Much' in his otherwise comprehensive account of his songwriting, *I Me Mine,* presumably because there was nothing much to say. A standard love story, the song describes how having been jilted, the lover feels everything will turn out all right in the end, as the girl simply loves him too much. If it had been written by John, he would undoubtedly have dismissed it as one of his throwaways.

**YOU LIKE ME
TOO MUCH**
Written:
Harrison
Length: 2' 38"
UK release:
Help! album,
August 6, 1965
US release:
Beatles VI album,
June 14, 1965

George's 'You Like Me Too Much' was one of the lesser tracks on the *Help!* soundtrack.

IT'S ONLY LOVE

John wrote 'It's Only Love' as an upbeat number, chock-full of the most clichéd rhymes and images, so it is little wonder people think this song is completely out of character. In the lyric, he describes how his girl lights up the night for him and yet he's suffering from butterflies in his stomach. The real problem is that he is in love.

It was one of the few Beatles' songs that John really hated. "I was always ashamed of that because of the abominable lyrics," he admitted in 1969. All the songs that John regretted having written were condemned on the grounds of their lyrics rather than their melodies, because he felt that he had produced platitudes rather than expressed any real feeling.

In this case, the song's shortcomings could have been a result of the pressure to come up with a further side of songs to complete the soundtrack album or simply that John was feeling at a low ebb.

George Martin and his orchestra recorded the composition as an instrumental using John's original working title of 'That's A Nice Hat'.

IT'S ONLY LOVE

Written:	Lennon/McCartney
Length:	1' 58"
UK release:	*Help!* album, August 6, 1965
US release:	*Rubber Soul* album, December 6, 1965

I'VE JUST SEEN A FACE

'I've Just Seen A Face' was a tune which Paul had been playing on piano for some time. He played it at family get-togethers back in Liverpool and his Auntie Gin loved it so much that it was dubbed 'Auntie Gin's Theme'. The George Martin Orchestra went on to record an instrumental version under this title.

Auntie Gin was the youngest sister of Paul's father Jim and would later get a mention in 'Let 'Em In' recorded by Wings, Paul's post-Beatle band.

I'VE JUST SEEN A FACE
Written:
Lennon/
McCartney
Length: 2' 07"
UK release:
Help! album,
August 6, 1965
US release:
Rubber Soul album,
December 6,
1965

A definite tonic to Paul's Auntie Gin, 'I've Just Seen A Face' was aired at McCartney family parties.

YESTERDAY

Paul woke up one morning in his top floor bedroom at the Ashers' home in Wimpole Street with the tune for 'Yesterday' in his head. There was a piano by the bed and he went straight to it and started playing. "It was just all there," he said. "A complete thing. I couldn't believe it."

Although at that point it had no lyric, Paul was worried that the tune itself might have been unconsciously plagiarized, and that what had seemed like a flash of inspiration may only have been a surge of recollection. "For about a month, I went round to people in the music business and asked them whether they had ever heard it before," he said. "Eventually it became like handing something in to the police. I thought that if no one claimed it after a few weeks then I would have it."

He then came up with the provisional title 'Scrambled Eggs' and began singing 'Scrambled eggs, Oh you've got such lovely legs', simply to get a feel for the vocal. This was a common practice and sometimes gave rise to interesting lines that were kept in the final version.

"We were shooting *Help!* in the studio for about four weeks," remembers Dick Lester. "At some time during that period, we had a piano on one of the stages and he was playing this 'Scrambled Eggs' all the time. It got to the point where I said to him, 'If you play that bloody song any longer I'll have the piano taken off stage. Either finish it or give it up!'"

Paul must have conceived the tune early in 1965, but it wasn't until June when he took a brief holiday in Portugal at the villa of Shadows' guitarist Bruce Welch that he'd completed the lyric. He then hit on the idea of using a one-word title – 'Yesterday'.

YESTERDAY

Written: Lennon/McCartney
Length: 2' 07"
UK release: *Help!* album, August 6, 1965
US single release: September 13, 1966
US chart position: 1

"I was packing to leave and Paul asked me if I had a guitar," says Welch. "He'd apparently been working on the lyrics as he drove to Albufeira from the airport at Lisbon. He borrowed my guitar and started playing the song we all now know as 'Yesterday'."

Two days after returning from Portugal, Paul recorded it at Abbey Road. The song startled pop fans at the time because it featured a string quartet with Paul as the only Beatle on the session. In America, it became a single and reached the Number 1 spot but, in Britain, it was never released as either an A or a B side during the group's career.

It rapidly became a pop standard, covered by everyone from Frank Sinatra to Marianne Faithfull. Nowadays, some 30 years on, it is still one of the most played tracks on American radio.

Although John claimed that he never wished that he had written it, he did admit that it was a "beautiful" song with "good" lyrics but argued that the lyrics were never resolved.

However, others have felt that its strength lies in its vagueness. All the listener needs to know is that it's about someone wanting to turn back the clock, to retreat to a time before a tragic event. The application is universal.

There has been speculation that in Paul's case the tragedy referred to was the death of his mother and the regret was over his inability to express his grief at the time.

Iris Caldwell remembered an interesting incident in connection with the song. She had broken up with Paul in March 1963 after a silly argument over her dogs (Paul wasn't too keen on dogs at the time) and, when he later called up to speak to Iris, her mother told Paul that her daughter didn't want to speak to him because he had no feelings.

Two and a half years later, on Sunday August 1, 1965, Paul was scheduled to sing 'Yesterday' on a live television programme, *Blackpool*

125

"Have you come far? And what do you do?" The Beatles encounter Princess Margaret at the London premiere of *Help!*, July 1965.

Night Out. During that week, he phoned Mrs Caldwell and said; "You know that you said that I had no feelings? Watch the telly on Sunday and then tell me that I've got no feelings."

In July 2003 the Liverpool writer Spencer Leigh made the discovery that there were both musical and lyrical similarities between 'Yesterday' and the Nat King Cole song 'Answer Me' (1953). The Cole song even has the lines 'Yesterday I believed that love was here to stay/ Won't you tell me that I've gone astray?' The response from Paul's office when the news broke was that the two songs were as alike as 'Get Back' and 'God Save The Queen'.

RUBBER SOUL

Although there had been hints of a new direction on the preceding albums, *Rubber Soul* marked a major period of transition. John would later call it the beginning of the group's 'self-conscious' period; the end of the Beatles' 'tribal child-like' stage.

Despite the cover, with its deliberately distorted photograph of the Beatles suggesting the perception shifts of LSD and marijuana, this wasn't a psychedelic album. Musically, however, it was an exploration of new sounds and new subject matter, introducing Paul on fuzz bass and George on sitar.

When producer George Martin played the piano solo back at double-speed to create a baroque sound, it was the first time that they'd tampered with tapes to create an effect.

There was a playfulness to *Rubber Soul* that extended from the wordplay of the title down to the 'beep beeps' and 'tit tits' of the backing vocals. Paul was quoted at the time as saying that they were now into humorous songs and both 'Drive My Car', with its role reversal, and 'Norwegian Wood', with its naive seduction scene, fitted into this category.

For a group that had only ever sung about love, 'Nowhere Man', a song about lack of belief, was a breakthrough: other songs like 'The Word' and 'In My Life' were only tangentially about boy-girl relationships.

The love songs of this evidenced a new maturity. Paul's 'We Can Work It Out', stemming from his own increasingly troubled relationship with Jane Asher, was a long way from the simple hope expressed in 'She Loves You' or 'I Want To Hold Your Hand'. John's 'The Word' pointed in the direction of the universal love that would

Although *Rubber Soul* saw the band getting more experimental, John and Paul were into 'humorous songs''.

later be the basis of songs like 'Within You Without You' and 'All You Need Is Love'.

Recorded over a four-week period in the autumn of 1965, *Rubber Soul* was released in December and became a chart-topping album in Britain and America. Four of the British tracks were left off the American album and these were replaced by two tracks from *Help!*

DAY TRIPPER

'Day Tripper' was written under pressure when the Beatles needed a new single for the Christmas market. John wrote most of the lyric and the basic guitar break, coming up with a riff that he later admitted was derived from 'I Feel Fine'. Paul helped on the verses and his bass riff owed something to the bass riff on Roy Orbison's 'Oh Pretty Woman' (1964).

In the summer of 1965, John and George had been introduced to LSD by a London dentist who slipped it into their coffee after an evening meal. In August, while in America, they took a trip of their own free will and from then on John confessed that he "just ate it all the time". 'Day Tripper' was a typical play on words by John, who wanted to reflect the influence of the growing drug culture within a Beatles' song. It was his way of referring to those who couldn't, like him, afford the luxury of being almost permanently tripped out. "It's just a rock'n'roll song," commented John. "Day trippers are people who go on a day trip, right? Usually on a ferryboat or something. But (the song) was kind of…you're just a weekend hippie. Get it?"

The song is about a girl who leads the singer on. His oblique description of the girl as a 'big teaser', was a knowing reference to the term 'prick teaser', a phrase used by British men about women who encouraged sexual arousal with no intention of having sex.

'Day Tripper' was released in both Britain and America as a double A-side single with 'We Can Work It Out'. It was the more popular song in Britain, reaching Number 1, but in America it peaked at five. The Beatles later said that 'We Can Work It Out' was their choice for the A side.

DAY TRIPPER
Written:
Lennon/McCartney
Length: 2' 49"
UK single release:
December 3, 1965
as double A-side
with 'We Can
Work It Out'
**UK chart
position:** 1
US single release:
December 6, 1965
as double A-side
with 'We Can
Work It Out'
**US chart
position:** 5
** Although 'Day
Tripper'/'We Can Work
It Out' was a double
A-side single, US chart
compilers calculated
their sales separately*

WE CAN WORK IT OUT

Despite its references to drugs, 'Day Tripper' (left) was aimed at the Christmas market.

**WE CAN
WORK IT OUT**
Written:
Lennon/McCartney
Length: 2' 15"
UK single release:
December 3, 1965
as double A-side
with 'Day Tripper'
**UK chart
position:** 1
US single release:
December 6, 1965
as double A-side
with 'Day Tripper'
**US chart
position:** 1

In October 1965, Jane Asher decided to join the Bristol Old Vic Company, which meant that she moved away from London to the west of England just at the time the Beatles were recording tracks for *Rubber Soul.* Her departure upset Paul and caused the first major rift in their relationship. As had been suggested in his songs, Paul's notion of a good woman then was someone who would be happy just to be around him. Jane's outlook was unusual at that time. She was not content to be a rock star's 'chick'. She was well-educated, independently minded and wanted, above all, to establish her own career.

In 'We Can Work It Out', Paul doesn't try to argue the merits of his case, but simply pleads with his woman to see things his way because he believes he is right and she is wrong. It was typical of Paul that, faced with what could be the end of a relationship, he didn't retreat sobbing to his room, but emerged with the positive slogan 'we can work it out'. The slightly downbeat middle eight, with its intimations of mortality, was added by John.

"You've got Paul writing 'we can work it out'," said John. "Real optimistic, and me, impatient, (with) 'Life is very short, And there's no time, For fussing and fighting my friend.'" The song was written at Paul's father's house in Heswall, Cheshire. The harmonium 'wash' was added in the studio as an afterthought and George Harrison suggested changing the middle-eight to waltz time.

DRIVE MY CAR

A first hearing of 'Drive My Car' might suggest that the Beatles are telling some 'baby' to drive their car, but closer inspection of the lyric reveals that it's the male narrator who is being asked to do the driving. He's trying to chat someone up, using that well-worn line, 'Well, what do you want to be?' – suggesting sexual favours in return for promises of career advancement.

The woman tells him that she wants to be a movie star – but then reverses the roles by saying that she might (and it is only might) agree to give him some love if he agrees to be her chauffeur. By the second verse it's the man who is pleading his case, arguing that his 'prospects are good'.

Paul remembered this song as the only one he got stuck on, the storyline being pulled together at the last minute with some help from John. When he arrived at Abbey Road on October 20, 1965, to record the song, the chorus was 'I can give you golden rings, I can give you anything, Baby I love you'. John dismissed this as "crap" and so the two of them huddled together to create an alternative and came up with 'Baby, you can drive my car', a tougher, more sexually-charged image

DRIVE MY CAR

Written:	Lennon/McCartney
Length:	2' 30''
UK release:	*Rubber Soul* album, December 3, 1965
US release:	*Yesterday And Today* album, June 20, 1966

"We've written some funny songs – songs with jokes in," said Paul, shortly after the band had finished recording 'Drive My Car'.

which in turn gave rise to the 'Beep beep beep beep yeah' background vocal. This was of course a playful reference to the 'yeah, yeah, yeah' that had become their signature shout and a gift to headline writers but it may also have been a nod to 'Beep Beep' by the Playmates (1958), a song that was a fixture on BBC's radio programming for children at the time that the Beatles started out.

John always agreed it was Paul's song with a bit of last-minute tuning and Paul said: "The idea of the girl being a bitch was the same but (the change) made the key line better." Two days after recording 'Drive My Car', Paul told a music magazine, "We've written some funny songs – songs with jokes in. We think that comedy numbers are the next thing after protest songs."

The bass line was patterned after Donald 'Duck' Dunn's playing on Otis Redding's 'Respect' (1965), which had been released the month before 'Drive My Car' was recorded.

NORWEGIAN WOOD

Although John was famous as the married Beatle he was not happily married. Nor was he faithful. He took advantage of backstage groupies, admitted to having been photographed on his hands and knees outside a Dutch brothel, and confessed to Cynthia in 1968 that he had had affairs. 'Norwegian Wood' was about one such entanglement. In language John later described as 'gobbledygook', the song details a seduction scene where again the woman appears to be the one in control.

The lyrics open with a boast about a girl John has 'had', but he quickly corrects himself by saying that it was she who 'had' him. She takes him back to her apartment and asks him to admire the furnishings that are made out of cheap Norwegian pine. After talking and drinking until two in the morning, she says it's time for bed. In the song, he makes his excuses and leaves for a night in the bathroom, but in reality the story obviously had a different ending because he said it had been written about an act of unfaithfulness, "without letting my wife know I was writing about an affair". John's friend Pete Shotton has said that it was about a female journalist that John was close to.

John began 'Norwegian Wood' in February 1965 while on a skiing holiday in St Moritz, Switzerland, with Cynthia, George Martin and George's future wife, Judy, but only came up with the basic tune and an opening couplet. He later asked Paul for help and Paul suggested that he should develop a story about a girl who leads a man on and ends with the man setting the apartment on fire as an act of revenge. Pete Shotton thought this could have referred to John's habit of burning furniture in the fireplace at Gambier Terrace

NORWEGIAN WOOD
Written:
Lennon/
McCartney
Length: 2' 05"
UK release:
Rubber Soul album,
December 3,
1965
US release:
Rubber Soul album,
December 6,
1965

in Liverpool when there was no money for coal. While he was there, John would sometimes ask guests to sleep in the bath, the memory of which may have prompted the line in 'Norwegian Wood' about sleeping in the bath.

Paul saw the song as a complete fantasy. The Norwegian wood of the title was suggested by the decoration of Peter Asher's room in Wimpole Street but to John it was definitely about a secret affair.

The track stood out on *Rubber Soul* for its use of sitar – it was the first time the Indian instrument had been used on a pop record. George Harrison had become fascinated with the sitar after coming across one while filming *Help!* in the Bahamas, and would later study under the Indian master Ravi Shankar.

John, Cynthia and Julian Lennon pose for a Goons-style slapstick photo, but the Beatle was unfaithful to his wife on a regular basis..

YOU WON'T
SEE ME

'You Won't See Me' was another song written by Paul during the crisis in his relationship with Jane Asher. By now, he was suffering the indignity of unanswered phone calls and other rejections. The dip in his romantic fortunes raised his writing to new heights because he now found he was the one in the vulnerable position. Paul had never seen life from this perspective. Throughout *Beatles For Sale* and *Help!*, he'd been dreaming up situations for his love songs but now, perhaps for the first time, he was writing from the heart.

As his relationship with Jane Asher turned sour, Paul's songs for her grew increasingly pained and vulnerable.

It was written as a two-note progression and Paul had the Motown sound in mind, particularly the melodic bass playing of James Jamerson, the legendary studio musician. Ian MacDonald in *Revolution In The Head* suggests that the specific model he might have had in mind might have been 'It's The Same Old Song' by The Four Tops.

'You Won't See Me' was recorded during the last session for *Rubber Soul*, by which time Jane was playing in *Great Expectations* at the Theatre Royal, Bristol.

YOU WON'T SEE ME
Written:	Lennon/McCartney
Length:	3' 22"
UK release:	*Rubber Soul* album, December 3, 1965
US release:	*Rubber Soul* album, December 6, 1965

NOWHERE MAN

Recorded on October 21 and 22, 'Nowhere Man' has the distinction of being the first Beatles' song not to be about love. John wrote it early one morning after a night out and it marked the beginning of his overtly philosophical musings.

'Nowhere Man' was always assumed to be either about a specific person (in her Hollywood exposé *You'll Never Eat Lunch In This Town Again*, Julia Phillips speculated that it was written about an entrepreneur called Michael Brown) or about an archetypal member of 'straight' society whose life had no purpose.

John said that he was the 'Nowhere Man' in question, and that desperation had driven him to it after he'd been writing solidly for over five hours, feeling that he wouldn't be able to complete another song for the album. "I'd actually stopped trying to think of something," he told Beatles' biographer Hunter Davies. "Nothing would come. I was cheesed off and went for a lie-down, having given up. Then I thought of myself as Nowhere Man – sitting in his nowhere land."

Like 'Help' it was about John's lack of self-worth and probably also about the fact that he felt both trapped in his marriage and trapped in the suburbs.

135

NOWHERE MAN
Written:
Lennon/
McCartney
Length: 2' 44"
UK release:
Rubber Soul album,
December 3, 1965
US single release:
February 21, 1966
**US chart
position:** 3

THINK FOR YOURSELF

Think For Yourself', a song written by George Harrison, is an admonition against listening to lies. Recorded just a few months before his engagement to Pattie Boyd, it was presumably not about his wife-to-be. "It must be about 'somebody' from the sound of it," he wrote in his book *I Me Mine*. "But all this time later, I don't quite recall who inspired that tune. Probably the government."

THINK FOR YOURSELF
Written:
Harrison
Length: 2' 19"
UK release:
Rubber Soul album,
December 3,
1965
US release:
Rubber Soul album,
December 6,
1965

George and Pattie Boyd on their wedding day, January 21, 1966.

THE WORD

THE WORD
Written:
Lennon/
McCartney
Length: 2' 43"
UK release:
Rubber Soul album,
December 3,
1965
US release:
Rubber Soul album,
December 6,
1965

Recorded two years after 'She Loves You' and two years before 'All You Need Is Love', 'The Word' marks the transition between the boy-meets-girl love of Beatlemania and the peace-and-harmony love of the hippy era.

Understood at the time as just another Beatles' love song, it was actually sprinkled with clues pointing to a song of a different kind. The love that John was now singing about offered 'freedom' and 'light'. It even offered 'the way'. He may even have been thinking of 'the word' in the evangelistic sense of 'preaching the word'.

In their classic study, *The Varieties Of Psychedelic Experience*, Masters and Houston found that not only did LSD often produce experiences of a religious nature, but it could provide people with the idea that "a universal or brotherly love is possible and constitutes man's best if not only hope". It was for this reason that 'love' became such a buzz word within the drug culture of the mid-to-late Sixties, John being one of the first songwriters to catch the mood. He later recalled the song as one of the Beatles' first 'message songs' and the beginnings of the group's role as cultural leaders expected to supply answers to social and spiritual questions.

John told *Playboy* that it was a song about "getting smart", meaning the state of realization which users of marijuana and LSD were claiming as theirs. "It's love," he said. "It's the marijuana period. It's the love and peace thing. The word is 'love', right?"

Appropriately, when John and Paul had finished writing it at Kenwood they rolled joints and wrote out a psychedelically decorated lyric sheet which John later gave to composer John Cage for his 50th birthday. A reproduction can be seen in Cage's book *Notations*.

MICHELLE

'Michelle' dates back to Liverpool days when Paul went to parties thrown by one of John's art tutors, Austin Mitchell. This was at a time when the intellectual life of the Parisian Left Bank was fashionable among art students and bohemianism was signalled by berets, beards and Gitanes. "Back in those days people would point at you in the street in Liverpool if you had a beard," remembers Rod Murray, who shared the Gambier Terrace flat with John and Stuart Sutcliffe. "If you had a beret, they would call you a beatnik. We liked Juliette Greco and everyone fancied getting in with Brigitte Bardot."

At one of these parties, a student with a goatee beard and a striped T-shirt was hunched over his guitar singing what sounded like a French song. Soon after, Paul began to work a comical imitation to amuse his friends.

It remained a party piece with nothing more than Charles Aznavour-style Gallic groanings as accompaniment until, in 1965, John suggested that Paul should write proper words for it and include it on the album.

Radio presenter Muriel Young, then working for Radio Luxembourg, can remember Paul visiting her at her holiday home in Portugal while he was working on it. This was probably during September 1965 when the Beatles took a month off between the American tour, which had finished on August 31, and the new album which was due to begin recording on October 12.

"He sat on our sofa with Jane Asher and he was trying to find the words," Muriel says. "It wasn't 'Michelle, ma belle' then. He was singing 'Goodnight sweetheart' and then 'Hello my dear', just looking for something that would fit the rhythm."

Nina Simone's phrasing on her hit 'I Put A Spell On You' helped to shape 'Michelle'.

Eventually, Paul chose to go with the French feel and to incorporate a French name and some French words. He spoke to Jan Vaughan, the wife of his old school friend Ivan Vaughan (the person responsible for introducing Paul to John), who was a French language teacher. "I asked her what sort of things I could say that were French and which would go together well," said Paul. "It was because I'd always thought that the song sounded French that I stuck with it. I can't speak French properly so that's why I needed help in sorting out the actual words."

Jan remembers that Paul first spoke to her about it when she and Ivan were visiting him at the Ashers' London home. "He asked me if I could think of a French girl's first name, with two syllables, and then a description of the girl which would rhyme. He played me the rhythm on his guitar and that's when I came up with 'Michelle, ma belle', which wasn't actually that hard to think of! I think it was some days later that he phoned me up and asked if I could translate the phrase 'these are words that go together well' and I told him that it should be 'sont les mots qui vont très bien ensemble'."

When Paul played the song to John he suggested the 'I love you' in the middle section, specifying that the emphasis should fall on the word 'love' each time. He was inspired by Nina Simone's recording of 'I Put A Spell On You', a hit in Britain during August 1965, where she had used the same phrase but placed the emphasis on the 'you'. "My contribution to Paul's songs was always to add a little bluesy edge to them," John said. "Otherwise, 'Michelle' is a straight ballad."

Instrumentally, Paul was inspired by the finger picking style of Chet Atkins as exemplified on 'Trambone' (1961) and was proud to have introduced the new chord of F7 #9 that he had been taught by Jim Gretty, the regular musical demonstrator at Frank Hessy's Musical Store in Liverpool.

"I remember George and I were in the shop when Gretty played it," said Paul. "We said 'wow! What was that, man?' And he answered, 'It's just basically an F, but you barre the top two strings at the fourth fret with your little finger. We immediately learned that and for a while it was the only jazz chord we knew."

MICHELLE
Written:
Lennon/
McCartney
Length: 2' 42"
UK release:
Rubber Soul album,
December 3,
1965
US release:
Rubber Soul album,
December 6,
1965

WHAT GOES ON

'What Goes On' was actually one of the four songs which the Beatles played to George Martin on March 5, 1963, as possible follow-ups to 'Please Please Me'. (The other three were 'From Me To You', 'Thank You Girl' and 'The One After 909').

Written by John some time previously, it was the only song Martin chose not to record on that day and it was forgotten until November 4, 1965, when it was taken out and dusted down for Ringo's vocal number. A new middle eight was added by Paul and Ringo; giving Ringo his first-ever credit as a composer. Asked in 1966 what exactly his contribution to the song had been, Ringo said: "About five words".

In America, it was released as the B side of 'Nowhere Man' in February 1966.

The Beatles revisited their achive of unused songs for 'What Goes On', which Ringo sang.

WHAT GOES ON

Written: Lennon/McCartney
Length: 2' 50"
UK release: *Rubber Soul* album, December 3, 1965
US single release: February 21, 1966 as B-side to 'Nowhere Man'
US chart position: 3

GIRL

Asked who the girl was in 'Girl', John said that she was a figure from a dream, the ideal woman who had not yet appeared in his life. "I always had this dream of this particular woman coming into my life," he said. "I knew it wouldn't be someone buying Beatles' records. I was hoping for a woman who could give me what I get from a man intellectually. I wanted someone I could be myself with."

However, the girl in the song seems far from his ideal. She's heartless, she's conceited and she humiliates him. Perhaps there are two girls in the song: the dream girl in the first half, whom he appears almost addicted to, and the nightmare girl in the second half who holds him up to ridicule.

The most John ever said about the song, though, was not to do with his images of women but his image of the Christian church.

In 1970, he revealed to *Rolling Stone* that the verse which asks whether she had been taught that pain would lead to pleasure, and that a man must break his back to earn leisure, was a reference to, "the Catholic/Christian concept – be tortured and then it'll be all

---

GIRL

Written:	Lennon/McCartney
Length:	2' 33"
UK release:	*Rubber Soul* album, December 3, 1965
US release:	*Rubber Soul* album, December 6, 1965

The bouzouki guitar of 'Girl'' is likely to have been influenced by a hit taken from the soundtrack of movie *Zorba the Greek*..

right." He added, "I was...trying to say something or other about Christianity, which I was opposed to at the time."

He could have been thinking of the Genesis account of the effects of Adam and Eve's disobedience, where Eve is told that "with pain you will give birth to children" and Adam is told that "cursed is the ground because of you; through painful toil you will eat of it all the days of your life."

Christianity, and in particular Jesus Christ, seemed to bother John. At the time of writing 'Girl', he was devouring books about religion, a subject that preoccupied him until his death, and four months later he gave the interview to Maureen Cleave containing his infamous comment that the Beatles were "more popular than Jesus".

The bouzouki style of guitar playing could have been influenced by the recent hit single 'Zorba's Dance' by Marcello Minerbi taken from the soundtrack of *Zorba The Greek*. The background vocals emulated the 'la la la la' chorus the Beach Boys used on 'You're So Good To me' (July 1965) but for a joke they sang 'tit tit tit tit' in the studio rather than the scheduled 'dit dit dit dit'. These borrowings show that the Beatles were as influenced by current chart music as they were by rare B sides and fifties r & b hits.

I'M LOOKING THROUGH YOU

Jane Asher's move to Bristol continued to preoccupy Paul. It meant that she was no longer readily at hand even though he was still living in her family home in Wimpole Street. As a young working-class man from Liverpool, he found it hard to come to terms with a girl who put her career before romance.

He later admitted to Hunter Davies that his whole existence so far revolved around living a carefree bachelor's life. He hadn't treated women as most people did. He'd always had a lot around him, even when he had steady girlfriends. "I knew I was selfish," he said. "It caused a few rows. Jane went off and I said, 'OK then. Leave. I'll find someone else.' It was shattering to be without her. That was when I wrote 'I'm Looking Through You'."

This was Paul's most bitter song so far. Rather than question his own attitudes, Paul accuses his woman of changing and holds out the thinly veiled threat of withdrawing his affection. Love has a habit, he warns, of disappearing overnight. He would later remember the song as having served to get rid of "some emotional baggage".

143

I'M LOOKING THROUGH YOU

Written:	Lennon/McCartney
Length:	2' 27"
UK release:	*Rubber Soul* album, December 3, 1965
US release:	*Rubber Soul* album, December 6, 1965

IN MY LIFE

Although John had been writing more obviously autobiographical songs for over a year now, it was with 'In My Life' that he felt he'd made the breakthrough that Kenneth Allsop had encouraged him to make in March 1964, when he suggested focusing on his own interior life.

Recorded in October 1965, the song was a long time in gestation. It started, John said, as a long poem in which he reflected on favourite childhood haunts by tracing a journey from his home on Menlove Avenue down to the 'Docker's Umbrella', the overhead railway which ran along Liverpool's dockside until 1958 and beneath which dockers would shelter from the rain.

Elliot Mintz, who was hired by Yoko Ono to carry out an inventory of all John's personal possessions after his death, remembers seeing the first handwritten draft of the song. "It was part of a large book in which he kept all his original Beatles' compositions," says Mintz. "He had already told me about how the song was written and that he considered it a significant turning point in his writing and, just as he had described to me, the song went on at great length and included lots of place names including Penny Lane."

In a later single-page draft of this rambling lyric, John listed Penny Lane, Church Road, the clock tower, the Abbey Cinema, the tram sheds, the Dutch cafe, St Columbus Church, the Docker's Umbrella and Calderstones Park. Although this fulfiled the requirement of being autobiographical, John realized that it was no more than a series of snapshots held loosely together by his feeling that once familiar landmarks were fast disappearing. The tramsheds were now 'without trams' and the Docker's Umbrella had been 'pulled down'. "It was the most boring sort of 'what I did on my holidays' bus trip

John felt that 'In My Life' represented a major leap in his bid to become a more raw, confessional writer.

IN MY LIFE

Written:	Lennon/McCartney
Length:	2' 27"
UK release:	*Rubber Soul* album, December 3, 1965
US release:	*Rubber Soul* album, December 6, 1965

song and it wasn't working at all..." he said. "Then I lay back and these lyrics started coming to me about the places I remember."

John jettisoned all the specific place names, and worked up the sense of mourning for a disappeared childhood and youth, turning what would otherwise have been a song about the changing face of Liverpool into a universal song about confronting death and decay. Here was a tough guy, who had been known to laugh at cripples and who poured scorn on the middle-class nature of his upbringing, but who was also a sentimentalist. Throughout his life, he kept a box of childhood mementos in his apartment and once wrote to his Aunt Mimi asking her to send him his Quarry Bank school tie.

He later told Pete Shotton that when he wrote the line about friends in 'In My Life', some of whom were dead and some of whom were living, he was thinking specifically of Shotton and former Beatle Stuart Sutcliffe, who had died of a brain tumour in April 1962.

The lyric bears a surprising resemblance to Charles Lamb's 18th-century poem 'The old Familiar Faces' which John could well have come across in the popular poetry anthology *Palgrave's Treasury*. The poem starts:

I have had playmates, I have had companions,
In my days of childhood, in my joyful schooldays:
All, all are gone, the old familiar faces.
Six verses later it concludes with:
How some they have died,
        and some they have left me,
And some are taken from me; all are departed;
All, all are gone, the old familiar faces.

The source of the melody to 'In My Life' remains in dispute. John has said that Paul helped out with a section on which he was stuck. Paul still believes he wrote it all. "I remember that he had the words written out like a long poem and I went off and worked something out on the Mellotron," he said. "The tune, if I remember rightly, was inspired by the Miracles." He was almost certainly referring to 'You Really Got A Hold On Me'.

On the track itself, the instrumental break was played by George Martin who recorded himself on piano and then played it back at double speed to create a baroque effect. John's opinion on the finished result was that it was his "first real major piece of work".

WAIT

WAIT
Written:
Lennon/
McCartney
Length: 2' 16''
UK release:
Rubber Soul album,
December 3, 1965
US release:
Rubber Soul album,
December 6, 1965

The Beatles don't appear to have had any great affection for 'Wait'. It was first recorded for *Help!* in June 1965, but not used, and was taken up again as the *Rubber Soul* sessions finished – but only because the album was a song short.

Written mostly by Paul, it's an all-purpose song about a couple who have been separated and now that they're back together everything's going to be all right. Paul's recollection is that it was written in the Bahamas during filming and that the late Brandon de Wilde, the child star of *Shane*, had watched as he wrote it.

Written in Nassau as the band filmed *Help!*, the unloved 'Wait' was a makeweight on the *Rubber Soul* album.

IF I NEEDED SOMEONE

'If I Needed Someone' was written by George for girlfriend Pattie, and grew out of a musical exercise using the D chord. "That guitar line, or variations on it, is found in many a song and it amazes me that people still find new permutations of the same notes," he said.

When Beatles' press officer Derek Taylor moved to Los Angeles and began to represent the Byrds, George asked him to pass a message to Byrds' guitarist Roger McGuinn saying that the tune to 'If I Needed Someone' had been inspired by two Byrds' tracks – 'The Bells Of Rhymney' and 'She Don't Care About Time'.

'The Bells of Rhymney' had been a track on the Byrds' first album *Mr Tambourine Man* that had come out in August 1965. 'She Don't Care About Time', written by vocalist Gene Clark, was the B side of the single 'Turn! Turn! Turn!' released in October 1965, the same month that 'If I Needed Someone' was recorded.

George admitted that his inspiration for 'If I Needed Someone' was two tracks by West Coast band the Byrds.

IF I NEEDED SOMEONE
Written: Harrison
Length: 2' 23"
UK release: *Rubber Soul* album, December 3, 1965
US release: *Yesterday And Today* album, June 20, 1966

RUN FOR YOUR LIFE

John developed 'Run For Your Life' from the line 'I'd rather see you dead little girl than see you with another man', which occurred towards the end of Elvis Presley's 1955 Sun single 'Baby, Let's Play House'. Indeed, John referred to this as "an old blues song that Presley did once" but in fact it only dates back to 1954 and was written by a 28-year-old preacher's son from Nashville named Arthur Gunter.

Gunter in turn had based his song on a 1951 country hit by Eddy Arnold, 'I Want To Play House With You', and had recorded it for the Excello label in late 1954. It wasn't a national hit but it was heard by Elvis who took it into the studios with him on February 5, 1955. When 'Baby, Let's Play House' reached Number 10 in Billboard's country chart in July 1955, it became the first Elvis record to chart nationally in America. Gunter's song was one of devotion. He wanted the girl to move in with him and the line which took John's attention was an indication of the depths of his feelings for her, not a threat.

However, in John's mouth the lines become threatening. If he sees his girl with anyone else she'd better run because he's going to bump her off. It was another revenge fantasy in the mould of 'I'll Cry Instead'. The singer explains his behaviour by saying that he's 'wicked' and that he was born with 'a jealous mind'; lines which contain intimations of later songs such as 'Jealous Guy' and 'Crippled Inside'.

Although it was the first track recorded for *Rubber Soul*, John always cited 'Run For Your Life' as an example of his worst work. It was written under pressure, he said and, as such, was a "throwaway song".

RUN FOR YOUR LIFE
Written:
Lennon/
McCartney
Length: 2' 18"
UK release:
Rubber Soul album,
December 3, 1965
US release:
Rubber Soul album,
December 6, 1965

149

REVOLVER

Revolver marked a significant development in the Beatles' sound, as well as the end of an era. After it, all their music was developed in the studio, unconstrained by considerations of whether the songs could be reproduced in concert. Now showing the obvious influence of contact with the emerging counter-culture and developments in avant garde art their work was appealing to a hipper audience. Encounters with the underground scene, along with the effect of psychedelic drugs, were to alter their perceptions both of themselves and of their music.

In a March 1966 interview with British teenage magazine *Rave*, Paul enthused about George's interest in Indian music and his own explorations of theatre, painting, film-making and electronic music. "We've all got interested in things that never used to occur to us," he said. "I've got thousands, millions, of new ideas myself."

Revolver was certainly an album brimming with new ideas. Eclecticism has since become common in rock'n'roll, but this was where it started. Not only did it involve musical styles ranging from a children's singalong to a psychedelic mélange of backward tape loops, it also presented a broad mix of lyrical concerns – death, taxation, pill doctors, lonely spinsters, sleep, ocean adventures and sunshine.

Yet, despite its experimental nature, *Revolver* was not inaccessible. 'Eleanor Rigby', 'For No One' and 'Here, There And Everywhere' were three of the most beautiful and popular songs Paul ever wrote. 'Taxman' and 'I Want To Tell You' were George's best compositions so far and John's dream-like 'I'm Only Sleeping' and 'She Said She Said' perfectly captured the mood of the times.

151

George's new interest in Indian music was a major influence on the groundbreaking sound of the *Revolver* album..

Released during what turned out to be their final tour, none of the 14 songs would ever be played on stage by the Beatles. They had become recording artists rather than performers, and were now happy to concentrate on the art of making records rather than having to squeeze their songwriting between touring and frequent appearances on film and television.

Revolver was released in August 1966 and made the top spot in both America and Britain. This was the last time that the British and American versions of a Beatles' album were to differ. Three of John's songs – 'I'm Only Sleeping', 'And Your Bird Can Sing' and 'Doctor Robert' – had already appeared in the US on the album *Yesterday And Today*.

PAPERBACK WRITER

The Beach Boys' *Pet Sounds* influenced the background harmonies of 'Paperback Writer'.

The Beatles' first single not to have a love theme ('Nowhere Man' had been the first song), 'Paperback Writer' was the story of a novelist begging a publisher's editor to take on his thousand-page book. Written by Paul in the form of a letter, it was startling at the time to hear a pop single on such an unusual subject.

British disc jockey Jimmy Savile, who then worked for Radio Luxembourg as well as BBC Television's *Top Of The Pops*, claims he was backstage after a show when Paul first conceived the idea for the song. John had been principal writer of the Beatles' last five singles and so it was generally agreed that it was Paul's turn to come up with something.

Savile recalled John asking Paul what he was going to do because there were only a few days left before they were due to record. "Paul told him that one of his aunts had just asked if he could ever write a single that wasn't about love," remembers Savile. "With that thought obviously still in his mind, he walked around the room and noticed that Ringo was reading a book. He took one look and announced that he would write a song about a book."

Paul has said that he had always liked the sound of the words 'paperback writer' and decided to build his story round them. The epistolary style of the song came to him as he drove down to Weybridge for a day's writing with John. "As soon as I arrived I told him that I wanted us to write it as if it were a letter," he said. Tony Bramwell recalls that the inspiration for much of the lyric came from an actual letter written to Paul by an aspiring novelist.

Paperbacks had caused a publishing revolution, making books available to people who would have found hardbacks too expensive to buy. Poet Royston Ellis, the first published author the Beatles had ever met when they played music backing his poetry in 1960, is convinced that Paul latched on to the phrase 'paperback writer' from his conversations with them. "Although I was writing poetry books then, if they asked me what I wanted to be I would always say 'a paperback writer' because that's what you had to be if you wanted to reach a mass market," says Ellis, who went on to become a writer of travel books and plantation novels. "My ambition was to be a writer who sold his books and made money out of it. It was my equivalent of their ambition of making a million-selling single."

As with many of Paul's songs, the lyric was driven more by the sound of the words than the logic of the story. Taken literally, it's about a writer who has composed a book based on a novel about a paperback writer. In other words, it's a novel based on a novel about a man writing a novel – which is in turn presumably based on a novel about a man writing a novel. The 'man named Lear' is probably a reference to Edward Lear, the Victorian painter who, although he never wrote a novel, did write nonsense poems and songs which John began to read when reviewers of *In His Own Write* suggested that he must have been an influence. The *Daily Mail* gets a mention because it was John's regular newspaper and copies would often be around the Weybridge house when they were writing. Stories from the *Daily Mail* would later be used as inspiration for two songs on *Sgt Pepper*.

The main musical innovation in 'Paperback Writer' was the boosted bass sound that allowed it to be used as a lead instrument for the first time. Paul was now playing a Rickenbacker and, through some studio innovations made by engineer Ken Townsend, the bass became the most prominent instrument on the track, bringing it into line with recent American recordings by Otis Redding and Wilson Pickett. The background harmonies were inspired by the Beach Boys' album *Pet Sounds* that had been completed by the end of March 1966 and an advance pressing brought to London by Kim Fowley in order to get it 'talked up' by influential people like the Beatles. John and Paul were given a preview at the Waldorf Hotel in the Aldwych. On part of the harmonies for 'Paperback Writer' the Beatles can be heard singing 'Frère Jacques' as a subliminal exercise in evoking childhood memories.

'Paperback Writer' was a Number 1 single in many countries including Britain, America, Germany and Australia.

PAPERBACK WRITER
Written:
Lennon/
McCartney
Length: 2' 18"
UK single release:
June 10, 1966
UK chart position: 1
US single release:
May 30, 1966
US chart position: 1

155

RAIN

In 'There's A Place' on the Beatles' first album, John had voiced the opinion that state of mind matters more than events 'out there'. In 'Rain', he returned to the theme but this time with the experience of psychedelic drugs as a subtext. On one level, it was a simple song about "people moaning because...they don't like the weather" as he once said. But on another level it was a song that recommended transcending the conventional categories of good and evil. In the same way that we should be indifferent to the weather, he feels that there is a need for people to rise above their circumstances. The use of 'I can show you' and 'Can you hear me?' indicated that John was starting to adopt the role of a leader.

'Rain' was the first Beatles' release that suggested new altered states of consciousness, not just in its lyric but in the music. The mournfully dragged-out vocal, the slowed-down instruments and the backward tape at the end were intimations of experiments to come.

Backward taping became a controversial issue in the rock industry during the Seventies and Eighties when some artists were accused

RAIN
Written: Lennon/McCartney
Length: 3' 02"
UK single release: June 10, 1966 as B-side to 'Paperback Writer'
US single release: May 30, 1966 as B-side to 'Paperback Writer'

'Rain' was the first song that saw the Beatles experiment with tape delay and effects,

of concealing hidden messages within their recordings. The Beatles had not done it to conceal messages but simply to suggest a mind free from conventional logic.

George Martin said that he came up with the idea experimenting on his own after the Beatles had left the studio. He played back his new effects to them the next day. John, who wrote 'Rain' at Kenwood, always claimed that he'd discovered the process trying to thread a demo tape of the song on his home recorder while high on marijuana. He was in such a disoriented state that he got the tape twisted and when he heard what sounded like an eastern religious chant coming from his headphones, he knew he had found a sound which accurately reflected his stoned consciousness.

TAXMAN

'Taxman' was written by George Harrison after he found himself in the British 'super-tax' bracket, which then meant paying 19 shillings and three pence (96p) out of every twenty shillings (£1) in tax. It has been suggested that the theme music to the TV series *Batman* may have been an influence – the 'taxman' chorus at the end of the song bears a resemblance to the 'Batman' chorus. This is possible because the first series starring Adam West as Batman started in January 1966 although it wasn't shown in Britain until May 1966, the month after 'Taxman' was recorded.

Until 1966, the Beatles' touring schedule had been so hectic that there had been no time to examine their accounts in detail. When they did get round to it, they discovered that they didn't have as much money as they had imagined. "We were actually giving most (of our money) away in taxes," said George. "It was, and still is, typical. Why should this be so? Are we being punished for something we have forgotten to do?" Ironically, in light of his later conversion to a religious view that stressed the futility of material things, George had always been the Beatle to mention money when asked about his ambitions.

John later said that he had a hand in the writing of 'Taxman' and he was bitter that George had neglected to mention this in the account of the song's composition in his autobiography, *I Me Mine*. John claimed that George phoned him up as he was writing it. "I threw in a few one-liners to help the song along, because that's what he asked for," he said "I didn't want to do it…but because I loved him...I just sort of bit my tongue and said OK."

Certainly the recorded version improved on George's rough draft, in which 'get some bread' was rhymed with 'before you're dead'. On

TAXMAN
Written:
Harrison
Length: 2' 39"
UK release:
Revolver album,
August 5, 1966
US release:
Revolver album,
August 8, 1966

George wrote 'Taxman' after discovering he was liable for 'supertax' and had to pay a 96% rate of income tax.

157

the first takes the background chorus was 'Anybody gotta lotta money/ anybody gotta lotta money/ anybody gotta lotta money?' sung at break-neck speed, but this was later changed to mention Prime Minister Harold Wilson and Leader of the Opposition Edward Heath. These two politicians shared the distinction of being the first living people to be named in a Beatles' song. Although they had never met Heath, they had met Wilson (a fellow Northerner) on several occasions and had each received MBEs in the honours list that Wilson approved after leading Britain's Labour Party to victory in 1964.

The Beatles – four enterprising young people with regional accents who came from mainly working class backgrounds – were just the sort of people Wilson wanted to encourage as part of his vision for a new classless Great Britain.

When the Trappist monk, poet and spiritual writer Thomas Merton (*Seven Storey Mountain*) heard 'Taxman' he wrote in his diary (June 10th 1967): "The Beatles' 'Taxman' is running through my head. They are good. Good beat. Independence, wit, insight, voice, originality. They take pleasure in being Beatles and I do not resent the fact that they are multi-millionaires, for that is part of it. They have to contend with that sneaky tax man."

ELEANOR RIGBY

As was the case with many of Paul's songs, the melody and the first words of 'Eleanor Rigby' came to him as he sat playing his piano. By asking himself what type of person would be picking up rice in a church where a wedding had been he was eventually led to his protagonist. She was originally going to be named Miss Daisy Hawkins as this fitted the rhythm.

Paul started by imagining Daisy as a young girl but soon realised that anyone who cleaned churches after weddings was likely to be older. If she was older, she might he a spinster and the church cleaning became a metaphor of her missed opportunities for marriage. He then based her on what he remembered of old people he'd known when he was running errands as a Boy Scout in Liverpool. "I couldn't think of any more so I put it away," he remarked.

Paul continued to mull over the song but wasn't comfortable with the name of Miss Daisy Hawkins. It didn't sound 'real' enough. Sixties folksinger Donovan remembered Paul playing him a version of the song where the protagonist was called Ola Na Tungee. "The words hadn't yet come out right for him," says Donovan."

He has always said that he settled on the name Eleanor because of Eleanor Bron, the leading actress in *Help!* Songwriter Lionel Bart, however, was convinced that the choice was inspired by a gravestone he saw in Putney Vale Cemetery in London as they sauntered through it together one day. "The name on the gravestone was Eleanor Bygraves," said Bart, "and Paul thought that would fit his song. He came back to my office and began playing it on my clavichord."

The surname originated when Paul came across the name Rigby in January 1966, while in Bristol visiting Jane Asher who was playing

'Eleanor Rigby' was called Daisy Hawkins, Eleanor Bygraves and even Ola Na Tungee before Paul finally settled on the title.

ELEANOR RIGBY

Written:	Lennon/McCartney
Length:	2' 07"
UK release:	*Revolver* album, August 5, 1966
US release:	*Revolver* album, August 8, 1966

the role of Barbara Cahoun in John Dighton's *The Happiest Days Of Your Life*. The Theatre Royal, home of the Bristol Old Vic, is at 35 King Street and, as Paul was waiting for Jane to finish, he strolled past Rigby & Evens Ltd, Wine & Spirit Shippers, which was then on the opposite side of the road at number 22. It had the two-syllable surname he was looking for to go with Eleanor.

The song was completed at Kenwood when John, George, Ringo and John's boyhood friend Pete Shotton crowded into the music room where Paul played it through. They each contributed ideas to flesh out the story. One of them suggested an old man rifling through garbage cans whom Eleanor Rigby could have a romance with, but it was decided that would complicate the story. A priest called Father McCartney was introduced. Ringo suggested that he could be darning his socks, an idea that Paul liked. George came up with a line about 'lonely people'. Paul reckoned that he should change the priest's name from Father McCartney because people would think it was a reference to his dad. A look through the phone directory produced Father McKenzie as an alternative.

Paul was then stuck for an ending to his story and Shotton suggested that he bring the two lonely people together in the final verse as Father McKenzie takes Eleanor Rigby's funeral and stands beside her grave. At the time, the idea was knocked down by John who thought that Shotton had missed the point but Paul, who didn't say anything at the time, used the scene to finish off the song, and later acknowledged the help he'd received.

Extraordinarily, sometime in the Eighties the gravestone of an Eleanor Rigby was discovered in the churchyard of St Peter's, Woolton, within yards of the spot where John and Paul had met at the church's annual summer fete in 1957. It's clear that Paul didn't get his idea directly from this gravestone, but it's possible that he saw it as a teenager and the pleasing sound of the name lay buried in his subconscious until called up by the requirements of this song. At the time he said: "I was looking for a name that was natural. Eleanor Rigby sounded natural."

In a further coincidence, the firm of Rigby and Evens Ltd, whose sign had inspired Paul in Bristol in 1966, was owned by a Liverpudlian, Frank Rigby, who established his company in Dale Street, Liverpool, in the 19th century.

As a single 'Eleanor Rigby' reached the top of the British hit parade but peaked at Number 11 in America.

Although the Beatles enjoyed unparalleled levels of success in 1966, John admitted that he was becoming increasingly lazy.

I'M ONLY SLEEPING

The first draft of John's lyric for 'I'm Only Sleeping', then called 'I'm Sleeping', was scratched on to the back of a letter from the Post Office, dated April 25, 1966, reminding him that he owed them 12 pounds and three shillings for an outstanding radiophone bill. Two days later the Beatles started to record it. It is clear from this first draft that he was writing about the joys of staying in bed rather than about a drug-induced dream state. His first opening line was 'Try to sleep again, got to get to sleep'.

John loved his bed. When he wasn't sleeping in it, he would be lying on it propped up by pillows writing or watching television. 'I'm Only Sleeping' celebrated the bed and its value as a place for contemplation. It also prefigured 'Watching The Wheels' on the *Double Fantasy* album. The more worrying truth, however, was that John was losing his grip on the Beatles, spending too much time either in bed or lazing around Kenwood. This indolent behaviour allowed Paul to grab the reins, something that was easier for him to do anyway because of his lack of family ties and the proximity to Abbey Road of his newly purchased London home.

It was the month before this recording that the *Evening Standard* ran Maureen Cleave's famous interview with John where he declared that "We're more popular than Jesus now; I don't know which will go first – rock'n'roll or Christianity." In the story Cleave noted: "He can sleep almost indefinitely, is probably the laziest person in England. 'Physically lazy,' he said. 'I don't mind writing or reading or watching or speaking, but sex is the only physical thing I can be bothered with any more'."

I'M ONLY SLEEPING
Written:
Lennon/
McCartney
Length: 3' 01"
UK release:
Revolver album,
August 5, 1966
US release:
Yesterday And Today album, June 20, 1966

161

LOVE YOU TO

Although 'Norwegian Wood' had featured sitar, it had been added as an afterthought. 'Love You To' was the first song written by George with the instrument specifically in mind. On this recording, he also featured tabla player Anil Bhagwat.

In his biography, *I Me Mine*, George recollected that he had used tabla and sitar on the basic track, overdubbing vocals and guitar at a later stage. However Mark Lewisohn, author of *The Complete Beatles Recording Sessions*, gained access to the original tapes and discovered that the sitar didn't appear until the third take and the tabla wasn't added until the sixth.

The song's working title was 'Granny Smith' – after the apple variety – simply because George couldn't think of anything better. As the words 'love you to' don't appear in the song, the eventual title is rather puzzling: perhaps 'love me while you can' might have been more appropriate as this sums up what the song is saying.

Despite writing 'Here There and Everywhere' (right) for Jane Asher, Paul denied they were to marry in 1966.

LOVE YOU TO

Written:	Harrison
Length:	3' 01''
UK release:	*Revolver* album, August 5, 1966
US release:	*Revolver* album, August 8, 1966

HERE, THERE AND EVERYWHERE

With things starting to look up again in his romance with Jane Asher, Paul wrote what is widely regarded as his greatest love song. Both John and Paul declared that it was one of their favourite Beatles' songs; Paul eventually re-recording it for use in his film *Give My Regards To Broad Street*.

Paul wrote 'Here, There And Everywhere' in June 1966 while sitting by John's outdoor pool. He'd arrived early for a writing session only to find John still in bed so he began to write alone. Wanting to set himself a structural challenge he built each verse of the song around the three adverbs in the title. When he recorded it he imagined the ethereal voice of Marianne Faithfull.

This song was the one of the album most obviously influenced by *Pet Sounds*. Paul had been particularly taken with the shimmering quality of 'God Only Knows' and wanted to write a number that captured the same mood.

HERE, THERE AND EVERYWHERE

Written:	Lennon/McCartney
Length:	2' 25"
UK release:	*Revolver* album, August 5, 1966
US release:	*Revolver* album, August 8, 1966

YELLOW SUBMARINE

The idea of writing a children's song about different coloured submarines came into Paul's head as he was drifting into sleep at the Asher home one night. This was to develop into 'Yellow Submarine', the tale of a boy who listens to the tall stories of an old sailor about his exploits in the 'land of submarines' and decides to go sailing and see for himself.

Between 1962 and 1965, the Beatles had obeyed the unwritten rules for writing pop singles: they should have love at the centre, last less than three minutes and be easily reproducible in concert. They were now enjoying seeing how many of these rules could be broken while still retaining the immediacy and excitement of commercial pop. 'Paperback Writer' had been their first non-love single; 'Eleanor Rigby' and 'Rain' were the first of their singles never to be played at a Beatles' concert and 'Yellow Submarine' was their first singalong song.

Paul used only short words in the lyric because he wanted it to be learned quickly and sung by children. While writing it, he visited Donovan at his flat in Maida Vale. "We were in the habit of just dropping in on each other," remembers Donovan. "I was just waiting for the release of my album *Sunshine Superman* and so we played each other our latest songs. One of the songs Paul played me was about a yellow submarine but he said he was missing a line or two. He asked me if I'd like to make a contribution. I left the room for a bit and came back with 'Sky of blue and sea of green, In our yellow submarine'. It wasn't an earth-shattering creation but Paul liked it enough to use it on the eventual recording."

The earliest takes of the song include the sound of marching feet before the song proper begins and Ringo intoning a spoken introduction.

Paul claimed 'Yellow Submarine' was "just a children's song" despite critics detecting druggy references – and Stanley Unwin.

The Stanley Unwin-inspired wordplay in the stanza suggests that this was written by John. 'And we will march 'til three the day/ To see them gathered there/ From Land O'Groats to John O'Greer with Stepney do we tread/ To see us yellow submarine/ We love it.' (Unwin may have had an effect on the album title itself. His first spoken-word recording, released in 1960, was called (Rotatey Diskers.)

Released as the flip side of 'Eleanor Rigby' in August 1966, the same month that *Revolver* came out, the rumour quickly spread that the yellow submarine was a veiled reference to drugs. In New York, Nembutal capsules started to be known as 'yellow submarines'. Paul denied the allegations and said that the only submarine he knew that you could eat was a sugary sweet he'd come across in Greece while on holiday. These had to be dropped in water and were known as 'submarines'. "I knew 'Yellow Submarine' would get connotations," said Paul, "but it really was a children's song."

YELLOW SUBMARINE

Written:	Lennon/McCartney
Length:	2' 40"
UK release:	*Revolver* album, August 5, 1966
US release:	*Revolver* album, August 8, 1966

SHE SAID
SHE SAID

Peter Fonda fell foul of an LSD-tripping John Lennon when the band threw a party at their Hollywood base.

When the Beatles visited Los Angeles in August 1965, they rented a house at 2850 Benedict Canyon for a week while they played dates in Portland, San Diego, the Hollywood Bowl and San Francisco.

One afternoon they threw a party, and Neil Aspinall, Roger McGuinn and David Crosby from the Byrds, the actor Peter Fonda and the *Daily Mirror* show business correspondent Don Short were among the guests. "Neil Aspinall was sent to escort me downstairs to the pool room," remembers Short, "because I was the only journalist on the premises. His job was to divert my attention from the fact that everyone else was taking acid."

Upstairs, out of Short's sight, everyone (except for Paul), was indeed tripping out on LSD. It was the first time John and George had deliberately taken the drug and they were anxious to have a good experience after the disturbing visions of their first, unintentional trip. Fonda had tripped out many times and saw his role as that of a guide. "I remember sitting out on the deck of the house with George, who was telling me that he thought he was dying," says Fonda. "I told

SHE SAID, SHE SAID

Written:	Lennon/McCartney
Length:	2' 37"
UK release:	*Revolver* album, August 5, 1966
US release:	*Revolver* album, August 8, 1966

him that there was nothing to be afraid of and that all he needed to do was to relax. I said that I knew what it was like to be dead because when I was 10 years old I'd accidentally shot myself in the stomach and my heart stopped beating three times while I was on the operating table because I'd lost so much blood.

John was passing by at the time and heard me saying 'I know what it's like to be dead.' He looked at me and said, 'You're making me feel I've never been born. Who put all that shit in your head?'"

Roger McGuinn felt that the idea had upset John because he was feeling insecure. "We were all on acid and John couldn't take it," McGuinn says. "John said, 'Get this guy out of here'. It was morbid and bizarre. We'd just finished watching *Cat Ballou* with Jane Fonda in it and John didn't want anything to do with any of the Fondas. He was holding the movie against Peter and then what he said just added to it."

Indeed, the earliest demo of the song (where it was called 'He Said, He Said') is far more aggressive than the final recording: 'I said, "Who put all that crap in your head?/ I know what it's like to be mad/ And it's making me feel like my trousers are torn"'. But John felt that as a song this was leading nowhere and abandoned it.

Although it came out of a real experience it meant nothing, he said. It was just a sound. But days later he picked it up again and tried to find a middle eight. "I wrote the first thing that came into my head," said John, "and it was 'when I was a boy', in a different beat. But it was real, because it had just happened."

Peter Fonda has no doubt about the origins of the song. "When I heard *Revolver* for the first time I knew exactly where the song had come from, although John never acknowledged it to me and I never mentioned it to anyone."

GOOD DAY SUNSHINE

'Good Day Sunshine' was written by Paul at John's house on a particularly sunny day. Paul admitted in 1984 that it had been influenced by the Lovin' Spoonful, the New York-based folk-rock group that had scored two American hits with 'Do You Believe In Magic?' and 'You Didn't Have To Be So Nice'. The group was distinguished by the lyrical, folksy tunes of founder member John Sebastian who later, as a solo artist, turned in a memorable performance in the *Woodstock* movie with 'The Younger Generation'.

The specific song that inspired Paul that day was 'Daydream', the Lovin' Spoonful's first British hit, which was in the Top 20 as the Beatles recorded *Revolver* in May 1966. Like 'Good Day Sunshine', 'Daydream' starts off with a choppy guitar beat before launching into a story of love-induced bliss heightened by beautiful weather: 'I'm blowin' the day to take a walk in the sun, And fall on my face on somebody's new-mown lawn'.

"One of the wonderful things the Beatles had going for them," says Sebastian, "is that they were so original that when they did cop an idea from somebody else it never occurred to you. I thought there were one or two of their songs which were Spoonful-oid but it wasn't until Paul mentioned it in a *Playboy* interview that I specifically realized we'd inspired 'Good Day Sunshine'."

'Daydream' itself was inspired by the Tamla beat on songs such as 'Where Did Our Love Go?' and 'Baby Love' that the Lovin' Spoonful heard while touring America with the Supremes. "I said, we gotta have a tune like 'Baby Love'," Sebastian remembers. "I wrote the song while trying to approximate the 'Baby Love' feel on one guitar.

GOOD DAY SUNSHINE
Written:
Lennon/
McCartney
Length: 2' 09"
UK release:
Revolver album,
August 5, 1966
US release:
Revolver album,
August 8, 1966

New York folk rockers the Lovin' Spoonful were flattered to learn they had influenced 'Good Day Sunshine'.

Sometimes you attempt to cop something and what you come up with is something very much your own."

The Lovin' Spoonful owed its foundation to a meeting between Sebastian and fellow guitarist Zal Yanovsky which took place at (Mama) Cass Elliot's house where the two men had been invited independently to see the Beatles debut on the *Ed Sullivan Show* in February 1964. "Seeing the Beatles that night crystallized the idea for us both of wanting to be part of a self-contained unit which wrote its own music," remarks Sebastian. "I eventually got to meet them in April 1966 (April 18th). John, Paul and George came to see us at the Marquee Club in London's Soho and it was that night that George had his first proper meeting with Eric Clapton. Unfortunately, we never got to play together because everyone was just so busy in those days. We had other meetings but we always seemed to be together because we were waiting for something else to happen.

"When they played Shea Stadium in New York in August 1966 I went backstage and had a few laughs with John who was beginning to look a lot like me. He was getting a lot of ribbing from the other Beatles about copying me. I always wished I could have spent more time with them."

AND YOUR BIRD CAN SING

John dismissed this song of his as "a horror" (1971) and "a throwaway" (1980) although it's hard to figure out what caused his dissatisfaction. The lyric was one of his most enigmatic and was probably a dig at Paul cloaked in the garments of poetry. After all, there had only been one previous Beatles' song title beginning with the word 'and' – Paul's 'And I Love Her'. Was John mocking this innovation and at the same time giving us a clue as to the target of his put-down?

The song is about someone who doesn't 'get' John, someone who does all the things that hip people do but isn't hip by nature. This was a gripe that he often made about Paul. The line 'You say you've seen seven wonders' could therefore be a reference to the first time the Beatles smoked pot in New York when Paul thought he had discovered the answer to all of life's big questions and wrote his insight on a piece of paper. When he read it the next morning all it said was 'There are seven levels'.

The period during which *Revolver* was recorded coincided with a time when Paul had a ravenous appetite for new cultural experiences

---

AND YOUR BIRD CAN SING

Written: Lennon/McCartney
Length: 2' 01"
UK release: *Revolver* album, August 5, 1966
US release: *Yesterday And Today* album, June 20, 1966

and this made John feel uneasy because he felt that, as an ex-art student, this was his territory. In April 1966 Paul was in print enthusing about the different forms of music he was getting into – Indian, classical, electronic – and bemoaning the fact that there simply wasn't time to listen to everything he wanted to. "The only thing to do is to listen to everything and then make your mind up about it." Could talk like this have led John to write, 'Tell me that you've heard every sound there is.'?

'And Your Bird Can Sing' shows signs of having been a typically sardonic put-down of Paul by the jealous and insecure John.

If this was a put-down, it 's unlikely that Paul was aware of it. During a session to add vocal overdubs he breaks up in hysterics when John deliberately mis-quotes his own lines and sings, 'When your bike is broken' instead of 'When your bird is broken' and then whistles the tune instead of singing.

FOR NO ONE

With its haunting melody and horn section, this was one of Paul's most beautiful songs. 'For No One' was written in a rented chalet half a mile outside the Swiss ski resort of Klosters, where he and Jane Asher spent a brief holiday in March 1966. He returned from Switzerland to work on *Revolver* and Jane began rehearsals for her role as the young Ellen Terry in *Sixty Thousand Nights* at the Royal Theatre, Bristol.

Through a series of flashbacks of their life together, the song captures the dawning realization that someone's feelings of love have disappeared. In an early interview, Paul said that it was all about his own experience of living with a woman when he was fresh from leaving home. The working title was 'Why Did It Die?' and he later admitted that it was probably written "about another argument" with Jane.

Paul and John worked on 'For No One' after Paul composed it on holiday before starting the *Revolver* sessions.

FOR NO ONE

Written:	Lennon/McCartney
Length:	2' 01"
UK release:	*Revolver* album, August 5, 1966
US release:	*Revolver* album, August 8, 1966

DOCTOR ROBERT

On their American visits the Beatles heard about a chic New York doctor who gave mysterious 'vitamin' injections. "We'd hear people say, 'You can get anything off him, any pills you want'," said Paul. "It was a big racket. The song was a joke about this fellow who cured everyone of everything with all these pills and tranquillizers. He just kept New York high."

Dr Robert was almost certainly Dr Robert Freymann, a 60-year-old German-born physician with a practice on East 78th Street. (The Dr Charles Roberts cited in some Beatles' books didn't exist. It was an alias used by the biographer of Warhol actress Edie Sedgwick, Jean Stein, to conceal the identity of another 'speed doctor'.) Known as Dr Robert or the Great White Father (he had a shock of white hair), Freymann was well connected to the city's vibrant arts scene. He had helped, among others, Theolonius Monk and Charlie Parker (whose death certificate he signed in 1955), and had a reputation for being generous with amphetamines. "I have a clientele that is remarkable, from every sphere of life," he once boasted. "I could tell you in ten minutes probably 100 famous names who come here." John, who wrote 'Dr Robert', was one of these famous names according to Freymann's daughter.

Initially prescribed as anti-depressants, amphetamines soon became a recreational drug for hip New Yorkers. One former patient of Dr Robert Freymann's, quoted in the *New York Times* in 1973, said: "If you want to make a big night of it you'd go over to Max's [Dr Max Jacobson] and then over to Freymann's and then down to Bishop's [Dr John Bishop]. It was just another kind of bar hopping." The film director Joel Schumacher, who used speed doctors in the Sixties,

DOCTOR ROBERT

Written:	Lennon/McCartney
Length:	2' 15"
UK release:	*Revolver* album, August 5, 1966
US release:	*Yesterday And Today* album, June 20, 1966

Crammed with their luggage in a small car, the Beatles arrive at a rainy London airport in August 1966 on the way to a US tour. It was to be their last.

agrees: "We thought of them as vitamin injections but then became speed freaks."

Administering amphetamines was not illegal at the time although regulations warned against prescribing 'excessive quantities' or giving the drug when it wasn't necessary. Dr Robert lost his licence to practise for six months in 1968 and, in 1975, was expelled from the New York State Medical Society for malpractice. Asked by the *New York Times* in March 1973 to defend his actions, he said: "the addicts killed a good drug". He died in 1987.

GOT TO GET YOU INTO MY LIFE

'Got To Get You Into My Life' was written by Paul who wanted to emulate the Motown sound recently developed by the writer-producer team of Holland-Dozier-Holland with The Supremes. It was the first Beatles' track to use brass.

John believed that by mentioning 'another kind of mind' in the lyrics, Paul was alluding to his drug experiences. He has since confirmed that he was. It was a hymn in praise of pot, disguised as a love song. It wasn't a woman that he needed every single day of his life but a joint.

On June 19, 1967, he was confronted by a British television news reporter who asked whether it wouldn't have been better if he'd kept his drug-taking private. "I was asked a question by a newspaper and the decision was whether to tell a lie or tell the truth," he said. "I decided to tell him the truth but...if I'd had my way, I wouldn't have told anyone because I'm not trying to spread the word about this...I'll keep it a personal thing if he does too. But he wanted to spread it, so it's his responsibility for spreading it. Not mine."

GOT TO GET YOU INTO MY LIFE

Written:	Lennon/McCartney
Length:	2' 30"
UK release:	*Revolver* album, August 5, 1966
US release:	*Revolver* album, August 8, 1966

I WANT TO TELL YOU

'I Want To Tell You', written by George, was about the frustrations of having things to say but being unable to articulate them. "It's about the avalanche of thoughts that are so hard to write down or say or transmit", he later said, adding that if he were to write the song again he would amend the bridge section which says: 'But if I seem to act unkind, It's only me, it's not my mind, That's confusing things' so that it was clear that his mind was responsible for the confusion. "The mind is the thing that hops about telling us to do this and do that. What we need is to lose the mind," explained George.

Appropriately for a song which was about not knowing what to say, 'I Want To Tell You' was recorded under the nonsensical title 'Laxton's Superb'; a name of an English apple, first suggested by engineer Geoff Emerick. It later became known as 'I Don't Know', after George Martin had asked George what he wanted to title it and had been given this answer.

I WANT TO TELL YOU
Written:
Harrison
Length: 2' 29"
UK release:
Revolver album,
August 5, 1966
US release:
Revolver album,
August 8, 1966

The Beatles at a press conference at New York's Warwick Hotel at the start of the final US tour in 1966.

TOMORROW NEVER KNOWS

As the last track on the album, and the clearest signpost of things to come, it's often assumed that 'Tomorrow Never Knows' was the last track recorded. In fact, it was the first. Certainly the weirdest and most experimental piece of music to appear under the Beatles' name at the time, this was John's attempt to create in words and sounds a suitable guide track for the LSD experience.

The words were borrowed, adapted and embellished from Timothy Leary's 1964 book *The Psychedelic Experience*, which was itself a poetic reinterpretation of the ancient Tibetan *Book Of The Dead*.

John had been sent the book by Barry Miles, who ran Indica Books in Southampton Row and was an influential figure on the British underground scene in the Sixties. He had an arrangement with the Beatles to send them significant books, magazines and newspapers to keep them up-to-date.

Leary, known as the High Priest of LSD, had spent seven months in the Himalayas studying Tibetan Buddhism under Lama Govinda. *The Psychedelic Experience* was a direct result of this period of study.

"I would ask Lama Govinda questions," says Leary, "and then I tried to translate what he said into something useful for people. *Book Of The Dead* really means 'Book Of The Dying' but it's your ego rather than your body which is dying. The book is a classic. It's the bible of Tibetan Buddhism. The concept of Buddhism is of the void and of reaching the void — that is what John captured in the song."

The words of the Tibetan *Book Of The Dead* were written to be spoken to a dying person in order to guide them through the states of delusion that come with the approach of death. Many people experienced the death of their egos while on LSD and so the words

TOMORROW NEVER KNOWS

Written:	Lennon/McCartney
Length:	2' 57"
UK release:	*Revolver* album, August 5, 1966
US release:	*Revolver* album, August 8, 1966

could be employed to keep trippers on track and protect them from the horrors. John is believed to have made a tape of Leary's words to listen to on headphones while he was tripping at home.

The working title of the track was in fact 'The Void', taken from Leary's line "Beyond the restless flowing electricity of Life is the ultimate reality – the void." Its eventual title was a Ringoism that John adopted because it added levity to what otherwise might have sounded like a bleak journey into nothingness.

The actual sound of the piece, which consists of tape loops made by each of the Beatles fading in and out, grew out of Paul's home experimentation on his tape recorder. "He had this little Grundig," says George Martin. "He found by moving the erase head and putting a loop on he could actually saturate the tape with a single noise. It would go round and round and eventually the tape couldn't absorb any more and he'd bring it in and play it."

John wanted it to sound like a chorus of Tibetan monks chanting on a mountain top." He said he wanted to hear the words but he didn't want to hear him," says George Martin. The result, which sounds as if John is singing at the end of a long tunnel, was achieved by feeding his voice through a Leslie speaker.

The Beatles relax by
a hotel swimming pool
as their 1966 US tour
gets underway.

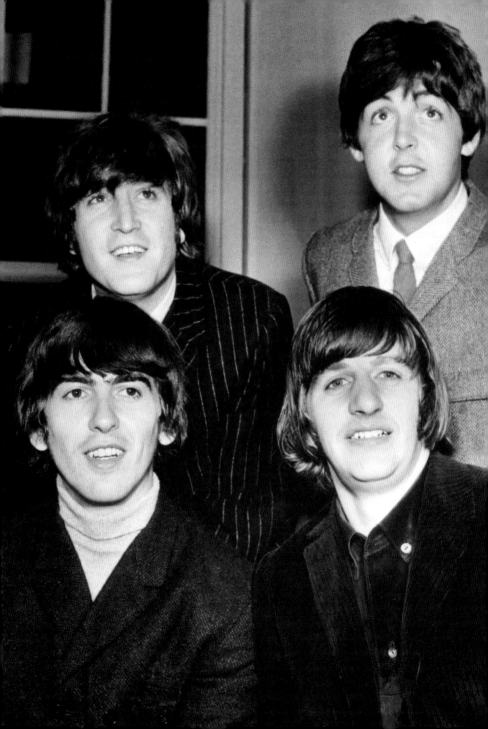

CHRONOLOGY

1940

July 7 — Ringo Starr born in Liverpool as Richard Starkey

Oct 9 — John Lennon born in Liverpool as John Winston Lennon

1942

June 18 — Paul McCartney born in Liverpool as James Paul McCartney

1943

Feb 25 — George Harrison born in Liverpool

1956

Oct 31 — Paul's mother, Mary, dies of breast cancer

1957

March — John Lennon forms the Quarry Men skiffle group with school friend Pete Shotton

July 6 — The Quarry Men play at the garden fete of St Peter's Church, Woolton, after which John is introduced to Paul by Ivan Vaughan

Oct 18 — After weeks of rehearsals Paul McCartney makes his debut with the Quarry Men

1958

Feb — George Harrison meets John and Paul and shortly afterwards is invited to join the Quarry Men

July 15 — John's mother, Julia, is killed in a hit-and-run accident

1959

Aug 29 — The Quarry Men play the newly opened Casbah Club which is run by Mona Best, mother of drummer Pete Best

1960

Jan — John's art school friend Stuart Sutcliffe joins the group on bass guitar. They start to be known variously as the Beatals, the Silver Beetles and the Silver Beats

May — London poet Royston Ellis uses the group to back him at a Liverpool reading. While staying with John and Stuart at their flat in Gambier Terrace, Ellis introduces them to the high produced by sniffing a broken-down benzedrine inhaler

May 10 — The Silver Beetles audition before Britain's top rock 'n' roll manager, Larry Parnes, and Liverpool's best known pop star, Billy Fury. They aren't offered the job of backing Fury but instead get a tour of Scotland playing for Johnny Gentle

May 20 — Silver Beetles begin seven-date tour with Johnny Gentle

July 9 — *Record Mirror* reveals that Royston Ellis is considering bringing a Liverpool group called the Beetles to London

Aug 12 — Pete Best auditions for the group and later joins on drums

Aug 17 — Now known as the Beatles, the group begins its first season in Hamburg, Germany – 48 nights at the Indra Club

Oct 4 — They then appear at the Kaiserkeller for a further 58 nights

1961

Feb 9 — The Beatles play the Cavern Club in Mathew Street, Liverpool, for the first time

April 1 — The Beatles return to Hamburg for a 13-week engagement at the Top Ten Club

June — The Beatles return to Hamburg and back English guitarist-vocalist Tony Sheridan

Aug	Polydor in Germany release 'My Bonnie' which is credited to Tony Sheridan and 'The Beat Brothers'
Sept	During a holiday trip to Paris, Paul and John change their hairstyles into what would later become known as the 'Beatle haircut' or 'mop top'
Nov 9	Brian Epstein visits the Cavern Club and sees the Beatles for the first time

1962

Jan 1	Fifteen audition track recorded for Decca Records in London
Jan 24	The Beatles sign a management contract with Brian Epstein
April 10	Stuart Sutcliffe dies of a brain haemorrhage while in Germany with his girlfriend Astrid Kirchherr
April 13	Start of a seven-week residency at the Star-Club in Hamburg
June 4	The Beatles sign a contract with EMI in England
June 6	First session at EMI Studios in Abbey Road with producer George Martin
Aug 16	Pete Best is dismissed as drummer
Aug 18	Ringo Starr joins the Beatles. The first John, Paul, George and Ringo concert is held at Hulme Hall in Birkenhead
Aug 23	John marries Cynthia Powell at Mount Pleasant Register Office, London
Sept 3	Second session at Abbey Road
Sept 11	Third Abbey Road session at which 'Love Me Do' is re-recorded with session drummer Andy White
Oct 5	British release of 'Love Me Do', the Beatles' first single
Nov 1	Return to the Star-Club, Hamburg, for 14 nights
Nov 26	Second single, 'Please Please Me', recorded at Abbey Road

Dec 18	Final return to club dates in Hamburg – 13 nights at the Star-Club

1963

Feb 2	Start of Beatles' first British tour. They support 16-year-old Helen Shapiro
Feb 4	Last lunchtime session at the Cavern
Feb 11	Debut album *Please Please Me* recorded in just over nine hours
Mar 9	Nationwide tour with American stars Tommy Roe and Chris Montez
April 8	Julian Lennon born as John Charles Julian Lennon in Liverpool
April 18	After an appearance at London's Royal Albert Hall, Paul meets teenage actress Jane Asher for the first time
Aug 3	The Beatles' final performance at the Cavern Club where they had played almost 300 times
Sept 11	Work starts on *With The Beatles* LP
Oct 13	An appearance on the top-rated British TV show *Sunday Night At The London Palladium* helps create the phenomenon the press later dub 'Beatlemania'
Oct 25	Start of a short tour of Sweden
Nov 1	The Beatles' Autumn Tour opens in Cheltenham, Gloucestershire
Nov 4	Royal Command Performance at Prince of Wales Theatre, London, before the Queen Mother and Princess Margaret
Dec 24	'The Beatles' Christmas Show' opens at the Astoria Cinema, Finsbury Park, London for a 16-night run

1964

Jan 16	An 18-day run at the Olympia Theatre, Paris, France
Feb 7	The Beatles fly to New York where they are greeted by 3,000 screaming fans
Feb 9	First appearance on the *Ed Sullivan Show* to

an estimated audience of 73 million

Feb 11   First American concert takes place at the
          Washington Coliseum

Mar 2   Shooting begins on *A Hard Day's Night*

Mar 23   John's first book, *In His Own Write*, is
          published

June 4   Beatles leave for a tour of Denmark,
          Holland, Hong Kong, Australia and New
          Zealand with Jimmy Nicol substituting for
          Ringo who is hospitalized with tonsillitis
          and pharyngitis

June 14   Ringo re-joins the Beatles in Melbourne

July 6   World premiere of *A Hard Day's Night* at
          the London Pavilion

July   John buys a home in Weybridge, Surrey

Aug 19   The Beatles' second visit to America but
          their first American tour. The first concert
          is at the Cow Palace in San Francisco

Aug 28   In New York City they are
          introduced to Bob Dylan
          and smoke marijuana for the first time

Oct 9   British tour begins in Bradford, Yorkshire

Dec 24   Another Beatles' Christmas Show opens
          for 20 nights at the Odeon Cinema,
          Hammersmith, London

1965

Feb 11   Ringo Starr marries Maureen Cox

Feb 23 – May 11 Filming *Help!*, the Beatles' second
                feature film

March – April   John and George experience LSD for
                the first time when a dentist friend spikes
                their after-dinner coffees

June 12   Each Beatle is awarded an MBE in the
                Queen's Birthday Honours list

June 24   John's second book, *A Spaniard In The
                Works*, is published

July 29   World premiere of *Help!*

Aug 14   Beatles arrive in New York for their second
                American concert tour

Aug 15   First appearance at Shea Stadium in
          Queens, New York. The attendance of
          almost 56,000 makes it the biggest pop
          concert ever

Aug 27   The Beatles meet Elvis Presley at his home
          in Bel Air

Aug   John and George take their second LSD
          trip in the company of actor Peter Fonda

Aug 31   Final concert of 1965 North American
          tour takes place at Cow Palace, San
          Francisco

Dec 3   The first date of what would turn out to
          be their final British tour

Dec 25   George gets engaged to Pattie Boyd

1966

Jan 21   George marries Pattie Boyd

Mar 4   John's interview with Maureen Cleave in
               which he claims that the Beatles are now
               "more popular than Jesus" is published in
               London's *Evening Standard*

April 6 – June 22 Recording *Revolver* at Abbey Road

June 24   Beginning of Far Eastern tour which goes
               from Germany to Japan and on to the
               Philippines

July   John's comments about the Beatles being
               bigger than Jesus are appear in the
               American magazine *Datebook* and trigger a
               Beatles backlash in the Bible Belt states

Aug 12   Final tour of America begins in Chicago

Aug 29   The last-ever concert performance by
               John, Paul, George and Ringo takes place at
               Candlestick Park, San Francisco

Sept 6 – Nov 6 John films *How I Won The War* in
               Germany and Spain

Nov 9   John meets Japanese artist Yoko Ono for
               the first time, in London

Nov 24   Beatles enter Abbey Road to begin
               recording *Sgt. Pepper's Lonely Hearts Club
               Band*

DISCOGRAPHY 1962-66

UK RELEASES

SINGLES

'Love Me Do'/'PS I Love You', October 5, 1962, Parlophone 45-R 4949.

'Please Please Me'/'Ask me Why', January 11, 1963, Parlophone 45-R 4983.

'From Me To You'/'Thank You Girl', April 11, 1963, Parlophone R 5015.

'She Loves You'/'I'll Get You', August 23, 1963, Parlophone R 5055.

'I Want To Hold Your Hand'/'This Boy', November 29, 1963, Parlophone R 5084.

'Can't Buy Me Love'/'You Can't Do That', March 20, 1964. Parlophone R 5114.

'A Hard Day's Night'/'Things We Said Today', July 10, 1964, Parlophone R 5160.

'I Feel Fine'/'She's A Woman', November 27, 1964, Parlophone R 5200.

'Ticket To Ride'/'Yes It Is', April 9, 1965, Parlophone R 5265.

'Help!'/'I'm Down', July 23, 1965, Parlophone R 5305.

'We Can Work It Out'/'Day Tripper', December 3, 1965, Parlophone R 5389.

'Paperback Writer'/'Rain', June 10, 1966, Parlophone R 5452.

'Eleanor Rigby'/'Yellow Submarine', August 5, 1966, Parlophone R 5493.

EPS

Twist And Shout, July 12, 1963, Parlophone GEP 8882 (mono)– 'Twist And Shout';'A Taste Of Honey'/'Do You Want To Know A Secret';'There's A Place'.

The Beatles' Hits, September 6, 1963, Parlophone GEP 8880 (mono) – 'From Me To You';'Thank You Girl'/'Please Please Me';'Love Me Do'.

The Beatles (No 1), November 1, 1963, Parlophone GEP 8883 (mono) – 'I Saw Her Standing There'; 'Misery'/'Anna (Go To Him)';'Chains'.

All My Loving, February 7, 1964, Parlophone GEP 8891 (mono) –
'All My Loving';'Ask Me Why'/'Money (That's What I Want)'/'PS I Love You'.

Long Tall Sally, June 19, 1964, Parlophone GEP 8913 (mono) –
'Long Tall Sally';'I Call Your Name'/'Slow Down'; 'Matchbox'.

Extracts From The Film A Hard Day's Night, November 6, 1964, Parlophone GEP 8920 (mono) – 'I Should Have Known Better';'If I Fell'/'Tell Me Why';'And I Love Her'.

Extracts From The Album A Hard Day's Night, November 6, 1964, Parlophone GEP 8924 (mono) – 'Any Time At All';'I'll Cry Instead'/ 'Things We Said Today';'When I Get Home'.

Beatles For Sale, April 6, 1965, Parlophone GEP 8931 (mono) – 'No Reply';'I'm A Loser'/'Rock And Roll Music';'Eight Days A Week'.

Beatles For Sale (No 2), June 4, 1965, Parlophone GEP 8938 (mono) –
'I'll Follow The Sun';'Baby's In Black'/'Words Of Love';'I Don't Want To Spoil The Party'

The Beatles' Million Sellers, December 6, 1965, Parlophone GEP 8946 (mono) –
'She Loves You';'I Want To Hold Your Hand'/'Can't Buy Me Love';'I Feel Fine'.

Yesterday, March 4, 1966, Parlophone GEP 8948 (mono only)– 'Yesterday';'Act Naturally'/'You

Like Me Too Much'; 'It's Only Love'.

Nowhere Man, July 8, 1966, Parlophone GEP 8948 – 'Nowhere Man'; 'Drive My Car'/'Michelle'; 'You Won't See Me'.

ALBUMS

Please Please Me, March 22, 1963, Parlophone PMC 1202 (mono), PCS 3042 (stereo) – 'I Saw Her Standing There'; 'Misery'; 'Anna (Go To Him)'; 'Chains'; 'Boys'; 'Ask Me Why'; 'Please Please Me'/'Love Me Do'; 'PS I Love You'; 'Baby It's You'; 'Do You Want To Know A Secret'; 'A Taste Of Honey'; 'There's A Place'; 'Twist And Shout'.

With The Beatles, November 22, 1963, Parlophone PMC 1206 (mono), PCS 3045 (stereo) – 'It Won't Be Long'; 'All I've Got To Do'; 'All My Loving'; 'Don't Bother Me'; 'Little Child'; 'Till There Was You'; 'Please Mister Postman'/ 'Roll Over Beethoven'; 'Hold Me Tight'; 'You Really Got A Hold On Me'; 'I Wanna Be Your Man'; '(There's A) Devil In Her Heart'; 'Not A Second Time'; 'Money (That's What I Want)'.

A Hard Day's Night, July 10, 1964, Parlophone PMC 1230 (mono), PCS 3058 (stereo) – 'A Hard Day's Night'; 'I Should Have Known Better'; 'If I Fell'; 'I'm Happy Just To Dance With You'; 'And I Love Her'; 'Tell Me Why'; 'Can't Buy Me Love'/'Any Time At All'; 'I'll Cry Instead'; 'Things We Said Today'; 'When I Get Home'; 'You Can't Do That'; 'I'll Be Back'.

Beatles For Sale, December 4, 1964, Parlophone PMC 1240 (mono), PCS 3062 (stereo) – 'No Reply'; 'I'm A Loser'; 'Baby's In Black'; 'Rock And Roll Music'; 'I'll Follow The Sun'; 'Mr Moonlight'; 'Kansas City'/'Hey-Hey-Hey!'/'Eight Days A

Week'; 'Words Of Love'; 'Honey Don't'; 'Every Little Thing'; 'I Don't Want To Spoil The Party'; 'What You're Doing'; 'Everybody's Trying To Be My Baby'.

Help! , August 6, 1965, Parlophone PMC 1255 (mono), PCS 3071 (stereo) – 'Help!'; 'The Night Before'; 'You've Got To Hide Your Love Away'; 'I Need You'; 'Another Girl'; 'You're Going To Lose That Girl'; 'Ticket To Ride'/'Act Naturally'; 'It's Only Love'; 'You Like Me Too Much'; 'Tell Me What You See'; 'I've Just Seen A Face'; 'Yesterday'; 'Dizzy Miss Lizzy'.

Rubber Soul, December 3, 1965, Parlophone PMC 1267 (mono), PCS 3075 (stereo) – 'Drive My Car'; 'Norwegian Wood (This Bird Has Flown)'; 'You Won't See Me'; 'Nowhere Man'; 'Think For Yourself'; 'The Word'; 'Michelle'/'What Goes On'; 'Girl'; 'I'm Looking Through You'; 'In My Life'; 'Wait'; 'If I Needed Someone'; 'Run For Your Life'.

Revolver, August 5, 1966, Parlophone PMC 7009 (mono), PCS 7009 (stereo) – 'Taxman'; 'Eleanor Rigby'; 'I'm Only Sleeping'; 'Love You To'; 'Here, There And Everywhere'; 'Yellow Submarine'; 'She Said She Said'/'Good Day Sunshine'; 'And Your Bird Can Sing'; 'For No One'; 'Doctor Robert'; 'I Want To Tell You'; 'Got To Get You Into My Life'; 'Tomorrow Never Knows'.

A Collection Of Beatles Oldies, December 9, 1966, Parlophone PMC 7016 (mono), PCS 7016 (stereo) – 'She Loves You'; 'From Me To You'; 'We Can Work It Out'; 'Help!'; 'Michelle'; 'Yesterday'; 'I Feel Fine'; 'Yellow Submarine'/'Can't Buy Me Love'; 'Bad Boy'; 'Day Tripper'; 'A Hard Day's Night'; 'Ticket To Ride'; ' Paperback Writer'; 'Eleanor Rigby'; 'I Want To Hold Your Hand'.

US RELEASES

SINGLES

"Please Please Me'/'Ask Me Why', February 25, 1963,Vee Jay VJ 498.

'From Me To You'/'Thank You Girl', May 27, 1963, Vee Jay VJ 522.

'She Loves You'/'I'll Get You', September 16, 1963, Swan 4152.

'I Want To Hold Your Hand'/'I Saw Her Standing There', December 26, 1963, Capitol 5112.

'Please Please Me'/'From Me To You', January 30, 1964,Vee Jay VJ 581.

'Twist And Shout'/'There's A Place', March 2, 1964, Tollie 9001.

'Can't Buy Me Love'/'You Can't Do That', March 16, 1964, Capitol 5150.

'Do You Want To Know A Secret'/'Thank You Girl', March 23, 1964,Vee Jay VJ 587.

'Love Me Do'/'PS I Love You', April 27, 1964, Tollie 9008.

'Sie Liebt Dich'/'I'll Get You', May 21, 1964, Swan 4182.

'A Hard Day's Night'/'I Should Have Known Better', July 13, 1964, Capitol 5222.

'I'll Cry Instead'/'I'm Happy Just To Dance With You', July 20, 1964, Capitol 5234.

'And I Love Her'/'If I Fell', July 20, 1964, Capitol 5235.

'Matchbox'/'Slow Down', August 24, 1964, Capitol 5255.

'I Feel Fine'/'She's A Woman', November 23, 1964, Capitol 5327.

'Eight Days A Week'/'I Don't Want To Spoil The Party', February 15, 1965, Capitol 5371.

'Ticket To Ride'/'Yes It Is', April 19, 1965, Capitol 5407.

'Help!'/'I'm Down', July 19, 1965, Capitol 5476.

'Yesterday'/'Act Naturally', September 13, 1965, Capitol 5498.

'We Can Work It Out'/'Day Tripper', December 6, 1965, Capitol 5555.

'Nowhere Man'/'What Goes On', February 21, 1966, Capitol 5587.

'Paperback Writer'/Rain', May 30, 1966, Capitol 5651.

'Eleanor Rigby'/'Yellow Submarine', August 8, 1966, Capitol 5715

ALBUMS

Introducing The Beatles, July 22, 1963,Vee Jay VJLP 1062 (mono), SR 1062 (stereo) – 'I Saw Her Standing There'; 'Misery'; 'Anna (Go To Him)'; 'Chains'; 'Boys'; 'Love Me Do'/'PS I Love You'; 'Baby It's You'; 'Do You Want To Know A Secret'; 'A Taste Of Honey'; 'There's A Place '; 'Twist And Shout'.

Meet The Beatles!, January 20, 1964, Capitol T-2047 (mono), ST-2047 (stereo) – 'I Want To Hold Your Hand'; 'I Saw Her Standing There'; 'This Boy'; 'It Won't Be Long'; 'All I've Got To Do'; 'All My Loving'/'Don't Bother Me'; 'Little Child'; 'Till There Was You'; 'Hold Me Tight'; 'I Wanna Be Your Man'; 'Not A Second Time'.

Introducing The Beatles, January 27, 1964,Vee Jay VJLP 1062 (mono; no stereo release) – 'I Saw Her Standing There'; Misery'; 'Anna (Go To Him)'; 'Chains'; 'Boys'; 'Ask Me Why'/'Please Please Me'; 'Baby It's You'; 'Do You Want To Know A Secret'; 'A Taste Of Honey'; 'There's A Place'; 'Twist And Shout'.

The Beatles' Second Album, April 10, 1964, Capitol T-2080 (mono), ST-2080 (stereo) – 'Roll Over Beethoven'; 'Thank You Girl'; 'You Really Got A Hold On Me'; '(There's A) Devil In Her Heart'; 'Money (That's What I Want)'; 'You Can't Do That'/ 'Long Tall Sally'; 'I Call Your Name'; 'Please Mister Postman'; 'I'll Get You'; 'She Loves You'.

A Hard Day's Night, June 26, 1964, United Artists UA 6366 (mono), UAS 6366 (stereo) – 'A Hard Day's Night'; 'Tell Me Why'; 'I'll Cry Instead'; 'I'm Happy Just To Dance With You'; plus two soundtrack instrumental cuts by George Martin & Orchestra/ I Should Have Known Better'; 'If I Fell'; 'And I Love Her'; 'Can't Buy Me Love'; plus two soundtrack instrumental cuts by George Martin & Orchestra.

Something New, July 20, 1964, Capitol T-2108 (mono), ST-2108 (stereo) – 'I'll Cry Instead'; 'Things We Said Today'; 'Any Time At All'; 'When I Get Home'; 'Slow Down'; 'Matchbox'/ 'Tell Me Why'; 'And I Love Her'; 'I'm Happy Just To Dance With You'; 'If I Fell'; 'Komm, Gib Mir Deine Hand'.

The Beatles' Story, November 23, 1964, Capitol TBO-2222 (mono), STBO-2222 (stereo) – 'Interviews plus extracts from 'I Want To Hold Your Hand'; 'Slow Down'; 'This Boy'/Interviews plus extracts from 'You Can't Do That'; 'If I Fell'; 'And I Love Her'/Interviews plus extracts from 'A Hard Day's Night'; 'And I Love Her'/ Interviews plus extracts from 'Twist And Shout' (live); 'Things We Said Today'; 'I'm Happy Just To Dance With You'; 'Little Child'; 'Long Tall Sally'; 'She Loves You'; 'Boys'.

Beatles '65, December 15, 1964, Capitol T-2228 (mono), ST-2228 (stereo) – 'No Reply'; 'I'm A Loser'; 'Baby's In Black'; 'Rock And Roll Music'; 'I'll Follow The Sun'; 'Mr Moonlight'/ 'Honey Don't; 'I'll Be Back'; 'She's A Woman'; 'I Feel Fine'; 'Everybody's Trying To Be My Baby'.

The Early Beatles, March 22, 1965, Capitol T-2309 (mono), ST-2309 (stereo) – 'Love Me Do'; 'Twist And Shout'; 'Anna (Go To Him)'; 'Chains'; 'Boys'; 'Ask Me Why'/ 'Please Please Me'; 'PS I Love You'; 'Baby It's You'; 'A Taste Of Honey'; ' Do You Want To Know A Secret'.

Beatles VI, June 14, 1965, Capitol T-2358 (mono), ST-2358 (stereo) – 'Kansas City'/ 'Hey-Hey-Hey-Hey!'; 'Eight Days A Week'; 'You Like Me Too Much'; 'Bad Boy'; 'I Don't Want To Spoil The Party'; 'Words Of Love'/ 'What You're Doing'; 'Yes It Is'; 'Dizzy Miss Lizzy'; 'Tell What You See'; 'Every little Thing'.

Help! August 13, 1965, Capitol MAS-2386 (mono), SMAS-2386 (stereo) – 'Help!'; 'The Night Before'; 'You've Got To Hide Your Love Away'; 'I Need You'; plus three soundtrack instrumental cuts by George Martin & Orchestra/ 'Another Girl'; 'Ticket To Ride'; 'You're Going To Lose That Girl'; plus three soundtrack instrumental cuts by George Martin & Orchestra.

Rubber Soul, December 6, 1965, Capitol T-2442 (mono), ST-2442 (stereo) – 'I've Just Seen A Face'; Norwegian Wood (This Bird Has Flown)'; 'You Won't See Me'; 'Think For Yourself'; 'The Word'; 'Michelle'/ 'It's Only Love'; 'Girl'; 'I'm Looking Through You'; 'In My Life'; 'Wait'; 'Run For Your Life'.

"Yesterday"…And Today, June 20, 1966, Capitol T-2553 (mono), ST-2553 (stereo) – 'Drive My Car'; 'I'm Only Sleeping'; 'Nowhere Man'; 'Doctor Robert'; 'Yesterday'; 'Act Naturally'/ 'And Your Bird Can Sing'; 'If I Needed Someone'; 'We Can Work It Out'; 'What Goes On'; 'Day Tripper'.

Revolver, August 8, 1966, Capitol T-2576 (mono), ST-2576 (stereo) – 'Taxman'; 'Eleanor Rigby'; 'Love You To'; 'Here, There And Everywhere'; 'Yellow Submarine'; 'She Said She Said'/ 'Good Day Sunshine'; 'For No One'; 'I Want To Tell You'; 'Got to Get You Into My Life'; 'Tomorrow Never Knows'.

BIBLIOGRAPHY

BOOKS ABOUT THE BEATLES

Bacon, David and Maslov, Norman. *The Beatles' England*. Columbus Books, London ,1982; 910 Books, San Francisco, 1982.

Baird, Julia. *John Lennon My Brother*. Grafton, London, 1988.

Beatles, The, Anthology, Cassell & Co., London, 2000.

Beatles, The, The Beatles Lyrics. MacDonald, London, 1969.

Bedford, Carol. *Waiting For The Beatles*, Blandford Press, Newron Abbot, 1984.

Braun, Michael. *Love Me Do*. Penguin, London, 1964.

Brown, Peter. *The Love You Make*. MacMillan, London, 1983.

Coleman, Ray. *Lennon*. McGraw Hill, New York, 1984.

Dalton, David and Cott, Jonathan. *The Beatles Get Back*. Apple, London, 1969.

Davies, Hunter. *The Beatles*. Heinemann, London 1968.

Elson, Howard. *McCartney: Songwriter*. W.H.Allen, London, 1986.

Evans, Mike (ed), *The Beatles Literary Anthology*, Plexus, London, 2004.

Freeman, Robert. *The Beatles: A Private View*. Pyramid, London, 1992.

Fulpen, H.V. *The Beatles: An Illustrated Diary*. Plexus, London, 1982.

Giuliano, Geoffrey. *Blackbird*. Smith Gryphon, London, 1991.

Goldman, Albert. *The Lives Of John Lennon*. Bantam Press, London, New York.

Gottfridsson, Hans. *The Beatles from Cavern to Star Club*. Premium Publishing, Stockholm, 1997.

Harrison, George. *I Me Mine*. W.H.Allen, London, 1980.

Harry, Bill (Editor). *Mersey Beat; The Beginnings Of The Beatles*. Columbus Books, London, 1977.

The Ultimate Beatles Encyclopedia. Virgin, London, 1992.

Henke, James, *Lennon Legend*, Weidenfeld & Nicolson, London, 2003.

Lennon, Cynthia. *A Twist Of Lennon*. W.H. Allen, London 1978.

Lennon, John. *In His Own Write*. Jonathan Cape, London, 1964.

Lewisohn, Mark. *The Complete Beatles Recording Sessions*. Hamlyn, London, 1988.

The Complete Beatles Chronicle. Pyramid, London, 1992.

McCabe, Peter and Schonfeld, Robert. *Apple To The Core*. Sphere Books, London, 1972.

McCartney, Mike. *Thank U Very Much*. Weidenfeld & Nicolson, London, 1982.

Mellers, Wilfrid. *Twilight Of The Gods*. Schirmer Books, New York, 1973.

Miles, Barry. *Paul McCartney: Many Years from Now*. Secker & Warburg, London, 1997.

Miles, Barry, *The Beatles: A Diary*, Omnibus Press, London, 2002.

Norman, Philip. *Shout*, Elm Tree, London, 1981.

Pedler, Dominic, *The Songwriting Secrets Of The Beatles*, Omnibus Press, London, 2003.

Quantick, David, *Revolution: The Making of the Beatles' White Album*, Unanimous, London, 2002.

Rolling Stone magazine. The Ballad Of John and Yoko. Michael Joseph, London, 1982.

Salewicz, Chris. McCartney: The Biography. MacDonald, London, 1986.

Schafiner, Nicholas. The Beatles Forever. MSF Books, New York, 1978.

Schultheiss, Tom. A Day In The Life. Pierian Press, Ann Arbor, 1980.

Sheff, David. The Playboy Interviews with John Lennon and Yoko Ono. New English Library, London, 1981; Playboy Press, Chicago, 1981.

Shepherd, Billy. The True Story of the Beatles. Beat Publications, London, 1964.

Shotton, Pete. John Lennon In My Life. Stein & Day, New York, 1983.

Stuart Ryan. David, John Lennon's Secret, Kozmik Press Center, New York, 1982.

Taylor, Alistair. Yesterday. Sidgwick and Jackson, London; Pioneer Books, Las Vegas, 1989.

Wenner, Jann. Lennon Remembers. Straight Arrow Books, San Francisco, 1971.

Wiener, Jon. Come Together: John Lennon In His Time. Faber & Faber, London, 1984; Random House, New York, 1984

GENERAL BOOKS

Anthony, Gene. Summer Of Love. Celestial Arts, Berkeley, 1980.

Buglioso, Vincent. Helter Skelter. Bantam, New York, 1974.

Fein, Art. The LA Musical History Tour. Faber and Faber, Boston, 1990.

Gaines, Steven. Heroes and Villains. MacMillian, London, 1986; New American Library, New York, 1986.

Gibran, Kahlil. Sand and Foam, 1927.

Gillett, Charlie. The Sound Of The City. Sphere Books, London, 1970.

Goodman, Pete. The Rolling Stones: Our Own Story. Bantam, New York, 1965.

Guinness Book of Rock Stars. Guinness, London, 1989.

Hotchner, A.E. Blown Away. Simon and Schuster, London, 1990.

Leary, Timothy. Flashbacks. Heinemann, London, 1983.

Maharishi Mahesh Yogi,. The Science of Being and the Art of Living. International SRM Publications, London, 1963.

Mascaró, Juan. Lamps of Fire, Methuen, London 1958.

Marsh, Dave. The Heart of Rock and Roll. Penguin, London, 1989; New American Library, New York, 1989

Oldham, Andrew Loog, Stoned, Secker & Warburg, London, 2000.

Smith, Joe. Off The Record. Sidgwick and Jackson, London, 1989.

Stein, Jean. Edie. Jonathan Cape, London, 1982.

Turner, John M. A Dictionary of Circus Biography (unpublished).

White, Charles. Little Richard. Pan, London, 1984.

Wolfe, Tom. The Electric Kool-Aid Acid Test. Bantam, New York, 1968.

Worth, Fred and Tamerius, Steve. Elvis: His Life from A-Z. Contemporary Books, New York, 1988.

Wyman, Bill. Stone Alone. Viking, London, 1990

INDEX

ACKNOWLEDGEMENTS

For interviews carried out specifically for this book I thank: Al Aronowitz, Diane Ashley, Marc Behm, Margo Bird, Tony Bramwell, Prudence Bruns, Iris Caldwell, Pattie Clapton, Allan Clarke, Maureen Cleave, Melanie Coe, Richard A Cooke, Nancy Cooke de Herrera, Meta Davis, Rod Davis, Pat Dawson, Richard DiLello, Royston Ellis, Peter Fonda, Johnny Guitar, Paul Horn, Kevin Howlett, Michael Hurll, Stephen James, Rod Jones, Tony King, Timothy Leary, Donovan Leitch, Julian Lennon, Dick Lester, John Duff Lowe, Angie McCartney, Roger McGough, Thelma McGough, Elliot Mintz, Rod Murray, Delbert McClinton, Denis O'Dell, Lucy O'Donnell, Alun Owen, Little Richard, Jimmy Savile, John Sebastian, Helen Shapiro, Don Short, Joel Schumacher, Lucrezia Scott, Derek Taylor, James Taylor, Doug Trendle, Dr John Turner, Jan Vaughan and Gordon Waller.

I also drew on past interviews conducted with Lionel Bart, Hunter Davies, John Dunbar, Cynthia Lennon, George Martin, Barry Miles, Spike Milligan, Roy Orbison, Ravi Shankar, Bruce Welch and Muriel Young.

For supplying information or setting up interviews I thank: Tony Barrow, Penny Bell, Gloria Boyce, Eleanor Bron, Lynne DeBernardis, Liz Edwards, Mike Evans, Peggy Ferguson, Roberta Freymann, Sarah Jane Freymann, Lynda Gilbert, Matt Godwin, Adrian Henri, Corinna Honan, Shelagh Jones, Andrew King, Martha Knight, Carol Lawrence, Mark Lewisohn, Brian Patten, Mrs Juan Mascaró, Robby Montgomery, Peter Nash, Iona Opie, Peter Rhone, Bettina Rose, Juliet Rowe, Phil Spangenberger, Alvin Stardust, Jean Stein, Sue Turner, Lisa Ullmann, Linda Watts and Paul Wayne.

I used facilities supplied by the following organizations: American Federation of Musicians, ASCAP, BMI, Beatles Shop (Liverpool), Bristol Library, Bristol Old Vic, British Library, Chiswick Library, Highland Bookshop and Wildlife Art Gallery (Traverse City, Michigan), National Newspaper Library, National Sound Archives, Nigerian High Commission, Performing Rights Society, Rochdale Library, Theatre Museum, UCLA Library and Westminster Library.

Finally, I would like to thank my agent Lisa Eveleigh who never gave up on the project and Piers Murray-Hill and Jonathan Goodman at Carlton Books.